Loyalty to country, respect for honor and courage, and love for one another are at the core of America's survival through pain and loss. G.I. Joe & Lillie *brings that message up close and personal through a story about one American G.I. family. I loved it. It moved me to tears. It reminds us all that America's core values of love, loyalty, and faith are built upon compassion and commitment within each family.*

> Dr. Laura Schlessinger, syndicated radio talk show host, best-selling author, and columnist

It was a wonderful story about your dad (G.I. Joe) and mom. It made me want to laugh and cry at the same time! I was flying over Germany during the time your dad was there. The guys on the ground had it rough. It is one of the best stories about hardship and pleasure that I have read!

> Chuck Yeager, Brig. Gen. USAF, Ret.

I've heard Joe Bonsall and the Oak Ridge Boys sing many times. Now I see that Joe writes as well as he sings — and presents a wonderful, true story in G.I. Joe and Lillie.

> Dr. Robert Schuller, Crystal Cathedral

Thousands of Americans left homes and families to fight against great evil during World War II. I was priveleged to know many of them. After reading this remarkable book, I also feel that I know G.I. Joe and Lillie, real Americans who met the challenge. My thanks to Joe Bonsall for sharing this story.

> Senator Bob Dole

Joe Bonsall's very touching tribute to his mom and dad reminds us of a generation of Americans who made it possible for all of us to live freely. The sacrifices of the "G.I. Joes and Lillies" during WWII, and their subsequent adjustment to normal life is a story with which we can all identify. It's honest and heartwarming, coupled with great humanity.

Dick Clark, dick clark productions
and legendary television personality

The story of G.I. Joe and Lillie is another poignant and inspiring reminder of the greatness of the World War II generation.

Tom Brokaw, NBC News

Joe, you are the man through whom your father lived the rest of his life. Your mom and dad were so proud of you . . . and so am I..

Duane Allen, The Oak Ridge Boys

This story exemplifies the integrity and character behind the American dream — even when the dream doesn't come true in the way you hoped it would.
A great story of enduring faith and true commitment.

Pat Robertson, The 700 Club,
Christian Broadcasting Network, Inc.

G. I. Joe & Lillie

Joseph S. Bonsall

G.I. Joe & Lillie

Remembering a life of love and loyalty

Joseph S. Bonsall

New Leaf Press

First printing: March 2003

ISBN: 0-89221-537-2
Library of Congress Number: 2002116492

Cover by Left Coast Design, Portland, Oregon
Author photo on cover by Jon Mir

Printed in the United States of America.

Please visit our website for other great titles:
www.newleafpress.net

For information regarding author interviews, please contact the publicity department at (870) 438-5288.

FOR: MOMMY

Contents

FOREWORD

For years George Bush and I have been huge fans of Joe Bonsall and the Oak Ridge Boys. We love their music. We love their love of country. And we love their deep faith and open belief in God.

Ours is a friendship that goes way back. The "Boys" love telling the story of the first time they met George. He was then vice president of the United States, and President Ronald Reagan had asked the Oaks to come perform on the South Lawn of the White House. As they were practicing that afternoon, they looked up to see a very excited George Bush charging across the lawn. He couldn't believe one of his favorite groups was playing right out his window.

That was the beginning of a wonderful friendship between the Bushes and the Boys and their wives. They came back to the White House and spent the night when George was president, and have come to visit us almost every summer at our home in Kennebunkport, Maine. They have been very loyal supporters, campaigning both for George and our sons, George W. and Jeb, and they have been there for us in good times and bad. We no longer just love their music, we love them.

Now after all these years of thinking we knew almost everything about them, we find out that in addition to having a great singing voice, Joe Bonsall also can write! It almost seems unfair that one person should have so much talent, but how lucky are we that he is willing to share both.

I laughed and cried when I read *G.I. Joe & Lillie*. It reminded me of when I fell in love with a man in uniform (I married him, too). It reminded me of how truly great the "greatest generation" was; how much they gave for their country, and for all the world, to be free. And it reminded me once again of the things that George and I hold most dear: faith, family, and friends, and love of our country.

Above all else, *G.I. Joe & Lillie* is a wonderful love story to be cherished by all.

Barbara Bush

PROLOGUE

The Oak Ridge Boys' buses and semi-truck pulled into Lancaster, Pennsylvania, early in the morning of March 29, 1999. We were excited about performing at the beautiful new American Music Theater that stood like a tall, proud beacon on Route 30.

On this cool and cloudy day, well over 5,000 people would arrive in tour buses, family cars, mini vans, and SUVs from all over eastern Pennsylvania. Moms and Dads, Grandmas and Grandpas, as well as children of all ages would soon arrive to hear the Boys sing their songs.

I have been singing with the Oak Ridge Boys since 1973, and I can honestly say that I rarely get nervous before a show. This particular concert would be unusually special, and I found myself more than a little anxious. Tonight, the Oak Ridge Boys would have some very special guests attending the show, and we all wanted to do our best for them.

Pennsylvania's Governor Tom Ridge had proclaimed this week to be "Honor Our Veterans Week" across Pennsylvania. In keeping with our own longstanding tradition of honoring those who have served our country, we invited over 30 veterans from the Southeastern Pennsylvania Veterans Center in Spring City to be our special guests.

Our entire group, Duane Allen, William Lee Golden, Richard Sterban, and myself, were waiting in the parking lot to meet the veterans. Soon the big blue bus arrived and parked in the space we had reserved for them beside our touring coaches. Right on cue, our band members and crew went into action helping the veterans into the theater.

From the beginning, our road manager, Timmer Ground, had taken a leadership role in this project. As he watched the veterans disembark, tears welled in his eyes the whole time.

I knew the reason for his emotions. His daddy, Gerald Philo Ground, was a member of the 82nd Airborne that parachuted behind enemy lines before the Normandy Invasion of D-day. Gerald was captured by the Nazis, and his bravery has been an inspiration to all of us for many years.

Each veteran received Oak Ridge Boys T-shirts and autographed pictures. It was our privilege to help the aides guide the elderly vets to their assigned seats and make sure they were comfortable and happy.

Most of these veterans had served in World War II, but some had fought in Korea and Vietnam. It was an honor for the Oaks to have them attend our show.

Among the veterans was a very special couple, sitting side by side in matching wheel chairs. In their mid-seventies, neither could walk. The wife suffered from diabetes and loss of eyesight, and the man appeared thin and frail.

She held on to her husband's left hand because the right one was paralyzed. He did not speak, but it was easy to see his excitement about being at the concert. When his wife reached over and kissed his cheek, all of the other veterans responded with cheers and smiles. At the veteran's home, they were known as G.I. Joe and Lillie.

We could actually feel the love that they had for each other, and it made them heroes in the eyes of their temporary friends. I use the word "temporary" because it was clear that many of these veterans would not be with us much longer. Our nation is losing this generation at an alarming pace, which is all the more reason to honor them *and* to thank them!

G.I. Joe was a decorated hero who lived a tough life before and after the war. Lillie, a Woman's Army Corp corporal, married him and stayed by his side no matter what kind of pain and setbacks came their way.

Their story is simply unbelievable, but true.

"He fought the war! He was a hero, and I won't throw him away like an old shoe," she would always say. With God by her side, she stayed true to her word. But, there is so much more to their story and I am about to share much of it with you in the pages ahead.

To honor G.I. Joe and Lillie, I wrote a song. I have not written many songs over the years, but I thought that this one fit the occasion. My singing partners agreed that it was worthy.

I would sing the song by myself with only an acoustic guitar for accompaniment. Donnie Carr, our illustrious guitar virtuoso, and I practiced the song backstage over and over again until I could sing it without crying. I actually got through it pretty well during the show although I still whimpered a little bit. I just couldn't help it.

There they were, looking up at me as I began to sing. G.I. Joe and Lillie surrounded by all of those veterans cheering and yelling for the Oak Ridge Boys. They were obviously having a great time and so was everyone else.

What a generation! They are all, most assuredly, the very best of America.

That night, in Lancaster, Pennsylvania, on the stage of the American Music Theater, I sang a song for G.I. Joe and Lillie, and I proudly write this story in their honor.

A heavy price was paid by all veterans. Because of their sacrifice, we are able to enjoy the freedoms of living in the greatest country on the face of the earth. We can only imagine the place in heaven that God is preparing for the likes of them.

I can still hear the song intro in my head and the feeling in my heart as I began to sing . . .

Let me hold you in my arms, handsome soldier,
Take my hand, for we are going home today.

May God continue to bless the United States of America.

PREFACE

S ince childhood, your author has had a fascination with many of the idiosyncrasies of war. I do not want to mislead you into thinking that I am a scholar on this or any other subject, for surely I am not.

I will admit, however, to obtaining most of my education as a result of constant reading, which I believe to be one of the greatest gifts that God has seen fit to bestow upon mankind.

One person's ability to write something that matters coupled with another's desire to read the written account and to learn and grow from the author's experience and knowledge is indeed a blessing. It is a wonderful system, and all it takes is some time.

It is the theory behind the Bible. God inspired certain men to write books. Along with the wonderful stories of the creation, the Flood, the many prophecies, and the life of our Lord and Savior, Jesus Christ, are some incredible love stories and war chronicles. The Bible is the greatest of all good reads, and I highly recommend it!

Perhaps my long-time interest in the history of war stems from the fact that I have known many who have fought for freedom on the battlefields of France, Korea, Iwo Jima, and Vietnam. Perhaps my fascination results from never having served in the military myself. Whatever the reasons, I have read books about conflict and combat since I was a little boy.

After my war comic book years, I graduated to books like *Guadalcanal Diary, Back to Bataan,* and *Hiroshima.* Throughout my early twenties, the Holocaust occupied my heart and mind. I read over 20 books about the death camps and the Nazi final solution to rid the world of those deemed to be undesirable. It constantly boggled my young mind.

I have read the accounts of many battles in various wars that were fought brutally from the land, sea, and air. I have visited museums and, like many of you, I have watched hundreds of television documentaries.

I have pondered heavily the evil mindset of men like Mussolini, Hitler, and, more recently, Osama Bin Laden and his band of evildoers.

I have wondered about the sheer audacity of Imperial Japan's attack on Pearl Harbor and the fanatical Al Qaeda group to attack New York City and Washington DC.

I have studied generals like Eisenhower, Patton, MacArthur and Swartzkopf. I have looked long and hard at various world leaders who governed during wartime. Many, like Roosevelt and Churchill, excelled during their time, and their names are etched in history. Others, like Lyndon Johnson, in my humble opinion, failed miserably.

I have read and digested more up-to-date books, such as *We Were Soldiers Once and Young, Flags of Our Fathers*, and *Black Hawk Down*. I learned a lot about our first battles in Vietnam, the Marines who raised the flag at Iwo Jima, and the conflict in Somalia in the early '90s from reading these books.

No Greater Love

What has always moved me the most? What has been the focus of my interest? What has brought many a tear to my eye and a swelling of my inner emotions? It is the sheer courage, willingness, and perseverance of the ordinary, individual American combat soldier.

They came from the cornfields, the prairies, the hills and hollers, the mountains, and the cement jungles to gather and fight for our right to live in a free country.

They were men of different colors and creed who fought together as the Army of One, as they are called today. Most of them were scared children in their late teens who enlisted on their own or were drafted by Uncle Sam. They endured basic training, followed orders, went where they were told to go, and shipped out via air, rail, and sea to dangerous and unfamiliar corners of the world.

With a gun in their hands and a picture of their family stuck inside their shirt pockets or battle helmets, off they went, knowing that chances were slim that they would ever return.

Their spilled blood has rained down from the skies, flowed into the seas, and soaked deep into the earth in places with far-off names like Iwo, Anzio, the Ardennes, Pork Chop Hill, and DaNang.

The grunt! The G.I.! The leatherneck. The soldier, sailor, airman, WAC, or WAVE, all rose above themselves to do something extraordinary. They heeded the clarion call to give everything that can be given for one's cause and beliefs.

Jesus called it "no greater love." Surely, there is no greater love than the love of a soldier, one for the other, when under fire in a foxhole or lost in a jungle or huddled up close inside the belly of a transport plane while waiting for a parachute jump into a ton of flack and shrapnel thousands of miles away from home.

Many, however, did not heed this call. Draft dodgers or conscientious objectors have stood for their beliefs, and I am certainly not worthy to judge them. They must be accountable for their decisions. Many, like myself, were certainly willing, yet did not serve because of a special situation, a health reason, or a technicality.

When Arab terrorists bombed our precious shores and killed thousands of innocent Americans, I wanted to have a dog in that fight. No arm of our nation's military, however, has a place for a Gospel-singing, country-crooning, old rock-and-roller in his mid-fifties with over one hundred million miles on his engine!

I pray daily that God will bless and keep these present-day young men and women who have heeded the new call to serve and to defend and, who are, even now, in harm's way, once again fighting a new kind of war against terrorism.

It is a vicious and important campaign to be certain. We will win this war but not merely because of our weaponry and superior technology. We will win because, once again, the enemy will underestimate the American will and spirit and question the resolve of our young warriors. As a result, our enemies will be punished severely!

Handcuffed to His Heart

As a side note, I must say that I have learned much from the books of Steven Ambrose about the individual experiences of the men who fought. Old veterans of long-ago battles seldom discuss what they went through in combat. If you have a battle veteran in your family, you know that is the case.

My late father-in-law, Albert Bell of Illinois, fought on Pork Chop Hill in Korea. Gerald Ground jumped out of planes over Germany as part of the 82nd Airborne, and another old friend, Sterling Lankford, fought the bloody battle of Iwo Jima as a *semper fi* blood-and-guts Marine.

Albert could tell you how cold he was. Gerald will recall his homesickness, and Sterling will talk about the practical jokes his comrades pulled on him. Not one of these incredible men, however, would talk about their horrendous experiences in combat. Those memories are buried deep within their souls and are perhaps best kept there.

When, however, they spend time with another wartime soldier, these men will share the moments when lives were lost and men lay bleeding and dying. It is then that tears will always fall. Tears *always* fall!

The emotion swells from down deep in the soldier's soul — not due to his own battle trauma — but because the old veteran remembers all the young friends who never came back.

The buddy who was right beside him, living, breathing, and laughing, and then — like the words of an old Bruce Springsteen song — "something slips"! Suddenly, he is gone.

The veteran is constantly overwhelmed to realize that he has lived out his life, earned a living, and raised a family. Yet, if not for the grace of Almighty God and a healthy dose of good luck, he would be resting on a green hill buried beneath a white cross like so many others who did not live to see the age of 21. A veteran carries these thoughts with him throughout his life like a piece of luggage that is handcuffed to his heart.

Necessary Enlightenment

To author Ambrose's credit, he managed to break down many barriers with the combat vets that he has interviewed. He persuaded them to open up and give an account of battle as seen through their own eyes and hearts. These are the personal stories of those men who fought the fight and witnessed the incredible hell of combat.

Steven Spielberg and Tom Hanks hit the nail on the head with *Saving Private Ryan*. The reality of that film is due to the fact that Mr. Ambrose was the technical advisor. Unlike many Hollywood efforts to capture war on the silver screen, this one got it right!

I cried like a little boy all the way through the movie. A light went on. I was there. I understood!

D-day veterans need never see that movie. They have already lived the hell! The rest of us, however, should see it, if only to get a snapshot for our mind's eye and file it away in our heart. You might place it inside a special folder and label it "Necessary Enlightenment."

World War II was a unique time for this country. The focus of every man, woman, and child was overseas. The soldiers came first. After all, they were the ones putting everything on the line for our American way of life, which is liberty and freedom for all.

We were fighting brutal enemies on two fronts. Our evil adversaries believed in an entirely different agenda for the future of mankind.

Imperial Japan in the Pacific and the Nazis in the European Theater were fighting for the cause of dictatorship and racial superiority. They were also motivated by pure greed and domination.

We could not let them win. These United States of America were just that — "united."

America's women worked in factories and raised their children, or they joined up as well. Our young men died daily as their children collected rubber, newspapers, and junk metal to support the war effort. Armored tanks, planes, and ammunition were hammered out of scrap metal scavenged by youngsters who, instead of playing ball, collected precious pieces of tin in Radio Flyer Red wagons.

Everyone in America worked together, pulled together, prayed together, cried and fought together for the purpose of winning this war and bringing our boys home.

Operation Overlord

The invasion of France on D-day, June 6, 1944, set in motion the bloody process of defeating Adolf Hitler and eventually ending the war in Europe.

In 1940, the British army, under the command of Lord Mountbatten, had the initial plan for an invasion of some kind against the German army. Until then, most of the war with Germany had been fought from a defensive posture. The Brits knew that this was no way to win a war.

American commanders and intelligence officers joined the conversations in 1941. All agreed that an invasion was the key to winning the war. Throughout 1942, while the war raged on, men sat around tables in secret meeting places in Casablanca, Quebec, Cairo, and Tehran and tried to figure out a way to pull off this massive mission. It was a logistical nightmare to be sure, and many disagreements arose between the British and the Americans as to how and where the attack should take place.

Finally, in the winter of 1943, everything began to fall into place. The commanders of the Allied forces of Europe, led by General Dwight David Eisenhower, began to formulate a final plan. His strategy had the potential to turn the tide of the war with Hitler's Nazis. It was the most ambitious undertaking ever devised in the history of warfare.

An invasion force of men, planes, and ships had been prepared. An armada of hundreds of thousands of men was waiting to cross the English Channel, hit the beaches of Normandy, and liberate France.

If the plan worked, the Allied army could seize the initiative and eventually take the war right to Hitler's doorstep in Berlin. To be successful, they needed a huge foothold. In these latter days of planning, the project was given a top-secret code name, Operation Overlord. The preparation for D-day would be well over a year, and there was much to do.

Uncle Sam Wants YOU!

About that same time, early on a warm and sunny spring day in May of 1943, a young and wiry 18-year-old street kid made his way north on Margaret Street in North Philadelphia to the U.S. Army Enlistment Center on Frankford Avenue. Tired of all the drinking and yelling at home, he realized he was probably going to get drafted anyway. In fact, he was surprised that he had not been drafted already.

His attitude was, "Let's get going! See the world! Uncle Sam wants YOU!"

G.I. Joe walked in the door, picked up a pen, signed his name, and in that moment, joined the United States Army!

CHAPTER ONE

THE NARROW ALLEY FROM HELL

I t is a long, long way from an alley in North Philadelphia to the Normandy beaches on the northern coast of France.

I say "alley" because the little street where G.I. Joe grew up was little more than just a narrow, concrete passageway. If you were to drive south on Margaret Street, away from the elevated commuter train station in the northern section of the city of Philadelphia called Frankford, you would come to a huge iron train trestle, where passenger trains, as well as long and heavy freight trains, cross above the street. To visit the home of G.I. Joe's childhood, one just stopped and took a hard left before going under the trestle.

The block-long, narrow alleyway was called Trenton Street. After climbing up a steep hill, the alley then straightened out and ran right alongside the railroad tracks for about 100 yards. Then it suddenly took another steep dive down the other side onto Orthodox Avenue.

Trenton Street had only four houses, and they all faced the tracks.

Picture a front door and 20 feet of a narrow front yard made up mostly of weeds and stones. The yard lay beside a potholed street, made of weathered concrete and cracked cobblestones. Only a layer of coal on the other side of the street provided a barrier for the four sets of horizontal railroad tracks. A train of some kind passed by every ten minutes or so, and its passing shook the dishes right off the shelves.

No wonder everybody in the house yelled at each other and alcohol abuse ran rampant. A train going by,

*G.I. Joe's parents
at the house on
Trenton Street*

or perhaps the grand opening of a pack of matches, provided as good of an excuse as any for G.I. Joe's father, Roy Sr., to get hammered.

G.I. Joe grew up during the late thirties and early forties with two older brothers, Roy Jr. and Elwin, and a younger sister, Viola. More often than not, their little house was also shared with Eleanor's mother. Grandma Longstreth's constant hollering and complaining added to the madhouse atmosphere.

The little green house on that narrow alley from hell must have been a lot like living in a crowded hole with a bucket on your head while ten guys beat on it with jackhammers. Sort of like . . . well, a foxhole!

A Mother's Love

During the war years, when much of America pulled together, G.I. Joe's family started to implode on a regular basis. G.I. Joe's dad was a little guy with a big complex who drank in order to escape the fact that he had been dealt a bad hand — although he never tried to change anything. He lost job after job and stayed drunk most of the time. In order to pay the bills, he depended on the money that trickled in from whatever pay his sons earned and the income brought home by Eleanor. She had a job cooking at a school cafeteria.

When Roy got drunk, he beat up on everyone in the house until Roy Jr. and Elwin grew bigger and stronger. Still, he continued to take out his frustrations on the youngest son. He constantly called G.I. Joe names and hit him with a belt. Roy's wife was a tough woman, outweighing Roy by about 60 pounds and would sometimes intervene.

G.I. Joe only loved his mother, although she seldom showed him much affection. No one else in the house seemed to matter. That bond remained strong in spite of all the chaos, and helped to keep him on an even keel. She cared just enough to provide an emotional cushion for a young man who wanted and needed to believe in his heart that his mom really loved him.

It was certainly not a Norman Rockwell painting.

Let Him Go!

G.I. Joe dropped out of high school and worked several jobs as an electrician's apprentice. He was handy with tools, a quick learner, and was able to bring some money home to place on the table. It was a way for him to prove to his mother and father that he could indeed do something right, despite the harsh words to the contrary that echoed constantly from Roy Sr., and his loudmouthed grandmother's constant hollering and screeching.

G.I. Joe came home from work one day and told his mother, father, and grandmother, "It's time for me to join the service and fight for my country."

Many guys that he had known from school and work had already answered the call of duty. At five feet and nine inches, and weighing only about 130 pounds, Joe had thin, yet muscular, arms. His legs had become strong from climbing up and down ladders every day, and he stood about two inches taller than his father.

Instead of pride and congratulations, G.I. Joe's announcement was met with violence. Stunned, the new recruit tried to duck the chair that Roy Sr. swung at his son's face.

It is unclear as to why this happened. Was it a deep feeling of failure and lack of self-worth? Could it have been jealousy, coupled with a fear that the boy might leave and actually accomplish something good in life, while the father never would?

Could the man have that much hatred for life itself, or was this as good a time as any to take out all of his own anger on his son one more time? Or do we just chalk it up to the good mix of Schmidts beer and Four Roses whiskey?

Whatever the case, a drunken Roy Sr. had to be just as shocked when his youngest son grabbed him by both shoulders and sat him right back in his smelly and stained living room chair.

"You'll never amount to anything!" Roy hollered as G.I. Joe turned and headed out of the house for the last time. He threw an empty whiskey bottle that missed the boy by a mile and kept up the tirade long after the door slammed shut.

"Go and join the army! Go on and fight the war. You'll probably get yourself killed on the first day! GO ON!!"

"Oh, just leave him alone, Roy," said Eleanor, although quite a bit late and without near enough conviction.

"Ahhhhh, let him go," screeched Grandma.

Going Anywhere

By 1943, Roy Jr. had already been drafted, and Elwin had joined up. Little sister Viola spent most of her time sitting in the weedy front yard, watching the trains go by and daydreaming about one day riding on one. *A nice seat looking out of a bright, sunlit window,* she thought, *and going somewhere. Anywhere. . . .*

G.I. Joe had shared that same daydream many times, and now he found himself aboard just such a train on his way to Maryland for basic training. That very train may have blown right by the old house and shook the dishes right off the shelf.

I like to believe that it did just that!

CHAPTER TWO

THIS MAN'S ARMY

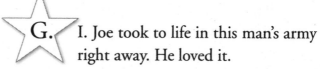

G. I. Joe took to life in this man's army right away. He loved it.

On August 16, 1943, G.I. Joe reported to Fort Meade, Maryland, for basic training.

Fort Meade was a major army training center throughout all of World War II. Between 1942 and 1946, approximately 3,500,000 men trained there. G.I. Joe was one of them.

He left Maryland as an anti-tank expert and would also qualify as a sharpshooter with an M1 rifle. As far as G.I. Joe was concerned, Fort Meade was a wonderful place, despite the physical demands and the rigorous education process.

Learning some of the technical information did not come easy to G.I. Joe. He met a lot of other boys who were riding in that same boat, however, and they helped each other quite a bit with the difficult study material.

Most of basic training was designed to whip these boys into good physical condition. As for G.I. Joe, he was glad to be doing something new, and felt optimistic about his chances of handling the challenges that would lie ahead. The underlying dread of war existed everywhere.

Although the regimen and discipline were tough, that didn't stop the men stationed at the various bases and camps around the country from having a good time. They liked to blow off steam built up by the mission that awaited them, and G.I. Joe was no different. The pressure was terrible, but G.I. Joe was one of the boys.

These young boys who made up the backbone of America would one day soon go to war and fight for her freedoms and liberties. Most of them were far away from their homes and families for the very first time, and they learned early on how to lean on and eventually love one another.

They would not only learn how to fight, they would also learn how to drink, smoke, and cuss. These vices were developed and finely tuned as a sort of diversion from the recruits' pure fear of what the future had in store for them.

In the 1940s, there was no "political correctness" to worry about. With a cruel irreverence, this melting pot of men from across America broke down every barrier and eventually brought them all closer to one another.

Whatever the origin of his religion or nationality, a soldier had to develop a thick skin, because somebody was going to unload on you. You had to learn to take it, and you also had to learn how to dish it out.

Welcome to the United States Army, boys. It was a unique buddy system to be sure and, somehow, it all worked.

After basic training, G.I. Joe's first set of orders was to report to Camp Barkeley, located just outside of Abilene, Texas. He was assigned to the 359th Regiment of the 90th Infantry Division.

The Fighting 90th, who were known simply as the "Tough Ombres," had a long and storied history. It began, ironically enough, fighting the German army in France during World War I!

After the Great War, they were disbanded. In this new conflict, the 90th was re-activated in Texas on March 25, 1942, as a motorized tank division.

Later on, in May of 1943, they were re-designated as an infantry division and would eventually ship overseas.

The "Tough Ombre" insignia

They would once again wear the monogrammed T-O insignia that had been created for them in 1918.

A Sense of Purpose

G.I. Joe arrived in Texas sometime in early October 1943. The men of the 90th had finished learning about tanks and the motorized theory of warfare. Now they were in the process of turning into a full-fledged infantry division.

The fresh and excited young soldier boy from Philadelphia had survived his grueling six weeks of basic training with flying colors. G.I. Joe was ready for the advanced instruction that would make him a true soldier.

"Those days at Camp Barkeley were the best times I had in the service," G.I. Joe said later.

The hot, dry Texas air, his new friends, and the excitement of thousands of young boys like himself all working together for one common cause gave him a sense of purpose and belonging.

It was nothing at all like where he grew up. Texas was hot, but the approaching autumn was taking the edge off the brutal summer that had preceded it.

The training at Fort Barkeley was hard and tough, with literally no breaks in the regimen. Many of the men couldn't take it. The constant training never let up. They had to learn close-order drills, extended-order drills, hasty field fortifications, field sanitation, map reading. The boys even mastered the fine art of potato peeling and dish washing.

Running for up to 25 miles across the hot Texas brush with a full load of gear was no picnic. The drill instructors kept reiterating over and over that the hard work would pay dividends when they found themselves far from U.S. soil and under enemy fire.

The United States Army wanted the new recruits in top physical condition and mentally prepared for any and every adversity that might come their way on the battlefield.

The Call to War

G.I. Joe was slowly being turned into an efficient fighting machine. When his time came, he would be a well-honed and combat-ready soldier. His expert marksmanship as well as his hard work ethic had paid off.

G.I. Joe earned himself a stripe and was promoted to the rank of private first class in the historic 90th Infantry. He felt good and was in the best shape of his young life. In July of 1943, while stationed at Fort Barkeley, he celebrated his 19th birthday. He was becoming one very Tough Ombre!

He almost lost that PFC stripe when he and several buddies got drunk one day on cheap Mexican booze and stole a tank. They drove it all over a Texas ranch until the military police finally caught up with them and placed the drunk and rowdy bunch under arrest.

The army was preparing these men for war, and it didn't have any time or tolerance for such actions. Luckily, a reprimand and a few nights in the brig were the only punishment handed out to G.I. Joe and his friends. They all got off easy because, after a few more days of advanced anti-tank tactical and weapons training, G.I. Joe's division would be shipping out.

The infantrymen believed that this was their call to war. When they boarded the troop train, they were told they would be heading farther west to the Arizona desert.

After a short stint at Fort Huachuca, Arizona, they traveled to Fort Ord (then known as Camp Ord) near Monterey, California, for more training.

As the days of learning and training quickly came to an end, the young soldiers knew they would soon be put to the ultimate test. The U.S. Army had determined that the men of the Fighting 90th Infantry were ready.

It was now time to enter the arena of war, where, when mistakes were made, men died. G.I. Joe had a premonition that his life was about to change forever. He was not wrong.

What We're Fighting For

The men figured they were heading to the Pacific from sunny California, but they figured wrong. The army, as usual, had different plans. The 90th would head directly east.

It was a subdued and somber bunch of Tough Ombres who boarded that troop train in California for a ride across the width of the nation to Fort Dix, New Jersey. There, final preparations would be expedited before the soldiers would, no doubt, be shipped overseas.

The men were exhausted and apprehensive, but they were all determined, to a man, not to show any fear. The trains were hot and very crowded. The men laughed, played cards, and stared out of the windows, but that specter of war and the unknown still kept right on tugging at them.

The passing countryside of the USA looked good to these boys. Most had never been away from home before joining the service. Many times people waving flags would line the tracks and wave at the troop trains. Young and old alike yelled words of encouragement. Sometimes, in many of the small towns and villages that dotted most of the middle of the nation, the turnout was so big that the trains would slow to a crawl as they passed through. Although the outpouring of patriotism made many of the boys even more homesick, it also lifted their spirits a bit to know that these folks cared about them. "Hey, this is what we are fighting for!" they told one another as the trains kept heading east.

Headed Somewhere

A month later, the men of the Fighting 90th waited patiently on the docks in New York City harbor as a light rain fell from the skies. They had no idea where they were heading except that their general destination was obvious: somewhere in the European Theater of Operations (ETO).

Due to trouble with their troop ship, departure was delayed for three days while repairs were made. Once again, the soldiers were herded aboard a train and sent back to Fort Dix, New Jersey.

G.I. Joe decided to hide out on the train and keep traveling on to Philadelphia. There he jumped off, went home, and paid a quick visit to his mother.

In the time he had been away, she did not write one word to him (and never would), but he still took a chance to see her. It was a short visit; a hello, a goodbye, a good luck, and soon he was hitchhiking back to Fort Dix.

Private First Class, G.I. Joe, was declared absent without leave (AWOL) for this little escapade. This time he *did* lose that stripe.

Finally, the young solders were herded into the deep hold of the converted cruise ship. While crossing the cold and rugged northern Atlantic Ocean, G.I. Joe threw up on a regular basis.

When the ship eventually docked in Liverpool, England, in early April of 1944, he was relieved to be back on land.

They boarded trains with the windows painted black, and rolled on eastward through an English countryside that was also blacked out and shrouded in darkness.

The German Luftwaffe had been pushed back out of the skies over England, but no one took any chances. Many of the troops were let off the trains in various quaint little towns north and east of the cities of Cardiff and Newport, Wales. There they set up camps and billeted in tents.

G.I. Joe, however, was a part of the third battalion of the 359th Infantry Regiment. His group received new and different orders.

The 359th was to be attached to the Fourth Infantry stationed in Devonshire, where they would undergo several more weeks of intense drills and training. They had been chosen to be the first wave to hit the beach at Normandy.

Invasion Fever

G.I. Joe and the men of the 359th had a severe case of "invasion fever." They knew that at any moment D-day could come. Still they trained.

In spite of the difficult training, the young soldiers were glad to have a new and different regimen. Mine detection, village fighting, assault on fortified positions, amphibious landing drills, beach assault, hedgerow fighting, demolition, and tactical maneuvers were drilled into them.

The men practiced transferring themselves as well as equipment from large Landing Craft Tank (LCT) to the smaller Landing Craft Infantry (LCI) or from LCIs to the even smaller Landing Craft Vehicle, Personnel (LCVPs).

They would attack and assault various beaches on the many islands east of Great Britain. These mock raids were physically draining and dangerous as well. Long before the real invasion ever took place, many men lost their lives on these training missions.

Soon, the waiting game started. They smoked cigarettes, drank English beer, played cards, and waited. Then, they waited some more.

Thousands upon thousands of fresh-faced, all-American boys waited along with their British army and Canadian counterparts for the words of General Dwight David Eisenhower. These words, this command, when finally spoken, would, in no time at all, echo down and through every line and chain of command.

These words would eventually change the very course of the history of the world, forever. G.I. Joe, one Tough Ombre, stared up at the stars and continued to wait.

At 9:45 p.m. on the evening of June 5, 1944, General Eisenhower had made up his mind to give the command. Then, when another torrential rainstorm came up, the general became apprehensive. After weighing the possible consequences of delaying any longer, he made his decision.

So it was at approximately 3:30 a.m. on the morning of June 6, 1944, the long-awaited command was finally given. The general simply turned to those assembled and spoke just three words, "Okay, let's go!"

The 101st and 82nd Airborne lifted off while 5,000 ships packed full of men, weapons, and machines prepared to steam across the British Channel.

The Normandy Invasion was on!

CHAPTER THREE

MEETING THE WORLD HEAD-ON

L illie Maude Collins, the 11th child of 11 children, was born to Kenneth and Otley Collins of Roanoke Rapids, North Carolina.

She had one sister named Blanche who eventually married a Washington and moved off to Richmond, Virginia. Blanche Washington! Now, there is a name for the movies or a southern novel! Blanche looked a lot like sister Lillie — only a little older.

Lillie's nine brothers grew up and stayed in North Carolina and either farmed like Papa or owned and managed RC Cola bottling companies from Raleigh to Winston-Salem.

The old home where Lillie grew up was very small. It was hard to believe that such a large family could have ever lived there. Constructed of rickety, gray wood, it had no indoor plumbing. Water was retrieved from an outside hand pump that, when vigorously man-handled, brought forth the coldest water on the planet.

The L-shaped house had a porch that ran all the way around one half of the L. Two swinging wooden seats hung from chains attached to the ceiling, and be-tween them was an old washer and ringer. Other pieces of furniture lined the porch as well, such as several chests of drawers, a small table with two chairs, and an over-stuffed couch. Today, we might call it "shabby chic." The Collins bunch, however, simply utilized every inch of space.

Since the farm had several barns, Lillie and her sis-ter would often wrap themselves in Mama's homemade quilts and sleep in a hayloft. The little house was always so cramped for space that sleeping up high in the barn was a delight for Blanche and Lillie. At night, it was so quiet that they could hear each other breathing.

Unlike G.I. Joe's Philadelphia home, there were no street sounds from cars driving by, no trains tooting, no loud cursing from two doors down, and no broken beer bottles crunching under foot.

In rural North Carolina, all the girls heard were the sounds of crickets, bullfrogs, and breathing.

The Collins Family

Lillie's brothers, with names like Frank, Tom, and John, spoke in the same sing-song, southern accent in which all their words ran together. Somewhat like a deep Southern drawl except that the cadence was quicker.

Lillie was known as "LillieMaude" which was spoken as all one word. The weather was "hotternheck." Daddy was "plowindafield." Frank was "sloppindahogs!"

You get the picture.

A dilapidated old outhouse with a top and bottom double door stood in the middle of a fenced-in field that the family shared with a cantankerous old mule. The trip to the outhouse had to be well planned by sidestepping the piles of manure and outsmarting the mule in order to reach the desired destination unscathed.

Once inside, the user could sit and relax while leaving the top door open to the elements, which was a necessity especially on hot days. If both doors were closed, the smell was overwhelming.

Then, you had to literally plan your way back out of there. Every trip was an adventure.

The strange part about the Collins family was the lack of love and affection shown to one another. By comparison, the situation was a lot like G.I. Joe's family in Philadelphia. How could that be, since no one in the Collins family drank or even cursed? The family all went to church twice on Sunday and once on Wednesday night for prayer and fellowship.

The son of Irish immigrants, Kenneth Collins was a quiet but gruff old man for the most part. He worked long and hard, feared God, and expected his children to do the same. Like most hard-working farmers, his hands were calloused and felt like leather. Kenneth Collins was also a strict disciplinarian and whipped up on the daughters as well as the sons with regularity to keep them in line. The only bad words ever spoken between him and Otley had to do with his hitting the kids, especially the girls.

He had a set of rules to govern this brood, and he stuck by them. He required everyone to work just as hard as he did if they expected to eat at his table and sleep beneath his roof. For the most part, none of them seemed to have a problem with it except for Lillie.

Leaving Home

Some words Lillie wrote many years later summed up her feelings on growing up in Roanoke Rapids: "I hated that farm. I hated it every single day. My father beat me for not working hard enough after I had been in that hot field for ten hours. Then he beat me again. It left big welts. I would say to myself, *Okay, Kenneth, you just wait!* I coulda killed him I think!"

When Lillie was in the ninth grade, Kenneth pulled her out of school so that she could pick more cotton. How ironic that G.I. Joe also dropped out of school in the ninth grade.

Not long after this incident, Lillie had her heart broken for the first time by a preacher's son named Leonard. He walked her home from church one day, and Lillie fell head over heels for him. He promised her that when they got a little older they would get married and he would take her far away from Roanoke Rapids.

The next year, he married someone else. It was too much for a 15-year-old farm girl who felt no one cared about her except her mother and saw nothing but a cotton field in her future. Besides, she wanted to be far away from the preacher's kid.

At the breakfast table the next morning, Lillie calmly made an announcement to all in attendance, "I am leaving home."

Ever since her brother Tom had joined the army, Lillie had been planning her own departure. Tom was now stationed overseas.

Lillie's mother, Otley, took this very hard and began to cry. None of the Collins brothers and not even sister Blanche said a word. In fact, most of them never stopped eating.

"Go on then," said her father. "One less mouth to feed!"

Lillie spent that whole day alone in the hayloft trying to sort things out.

Later that evening, as she was sitting in a swinging chair on the porch, her mother heard the sound of the chain creaking. She opened the screen door, walked out onto the porch, and sat beside her youngest child.

"Can't say as I blame you much, Lillie Maude, for feeling the way you do," whispered Otley Collins as she put her arm around Lillie's shoulder. "There's more to life than all of this. At least, I always thought so. I have thought about leaving this place many times, too, but a woman has to stay loyal to her family. That's God's will."

"I'll miss you, Mama," Lillie cried.

"Now you listen to me, Lillie Maude. You do what you have to do. Just remember I will always love you, and I will be right here on this porch to welcome you home. I'll pray for you every night."

Otley kissed her daughter on the forehead and went on to bed.

That night Lillie crawled out of her bedroom window, crossed the field and kept on walking. She stuck out her thumb and hitched a ride all the way to Baltimore, Maryland. It was late in the summer of 1943 when a 16-year-old Lillie prepared to meet the world head on.

Making Bombers

Lillie arrived in Baltimore and took a long walk around town. When she came upon a bunch of young girls who were all standing in a line, she asked, "What are you waiting for?"

"We're signing up for a camp," a girl explained, "that will teach us the skills required to get a job in a factory making airplanes."

Well now, this sounded pretty good, so Lillie joined the line and signed up. She spent six weeks in this training camp and loved every bit of it. She made friends with a girl named Juanita who was raised in Detroit,

Michigan. Juanita convinced Lillie to go to Detroit with her after they received their diploma.

Lillie's friend Juanita

In the meantime, a letter from Lillie's mother revealed that Leonard had been drafted and his wife wanted a divorce. Lillie wrote back and told her mother to have him call her in Detroit when he got home from basic training.

Lillie and Juanita moved into a boarding home in Detroit and they both got a job at a defense plant (most likely Willow River in nearby Ypsilanti, Michigan). During World War II, almost 8,700 B–24 as well as B-27 "Liberator" bombers were built at Willow Run. During its peak production, the plant employed 42,000 people, including "Rosie the Riveter."

It was at Willow Run that a young lady posed for a poster and became known all over the country as Rosie. That likeness of Rosie the Riveter became a symbol for the American women who took over the factory jobs left vacant by the men shipped to fight overseas.

Lillie worked as a machine operator making cockpit parts for B-24s. She also spent time on the assembly lines riveting. Although the work was very hard, Lillie found it exciting and fulfilling. In fact, her time spent working and living in Detroit may have been some of the happiest days of her life. "It sure beats pickin' cotton!" she wrote to her mother.

She would also write in her memoirs: "I worked hard at the defense plant, and I loved it. I felt I was finally doing something with my life. I knew I was helping with the war effort, and I prayed every night that God would bless and keep our boys overseas. When I was working on a part, I would wonder where it would end up. It would make me cry."

Farewell

One night, Leonard called. "I am getting a medical leave from the army," he told Lillie. "You know that I am now divorced. I'd like to come to Detroit and be with you."

Lillie was so happy about this and lined up a job for him at the defense plant, but he never called back. Days later, Lillie found out from her sister Blanche that Leonard had married someone else — again!

Once again her heart was broken. She cried for days, vowing all the while that there was no way under heaven that she would ever fall in love again. Not ever!

Lillie decided that she was going to enjoy life to the fullest and have as much fun as possible. Still, she never drank or smoked or ran around with the wrong crowd.

Lillie wrote in her diary, "I stayed true to God throughout my whole life and honored Him in everything I did."

In Detroit, Juanita and Lillie would go dancing and to the movies, but it was all good clean fun. Lillie's favorite movie was *Hollywood Canteen*. Released in 1944, it starred the Andrews Sisters, Jack Benny, Joan Crawford, and Bette Davis.

The girls sat through the movie three times and went back the next day to watch it again.

My father would have just flipped! Lillie remembered thinking.

Lillie dated a few guys now and then but never let them get close. She started meeting a lot of the soldiers who were home on leave and was intrigued with the stories they shared about the fighting and the sacrifice.

The war was first and foremost on her mind all the time, and she started to feel that she wanted to do more. She picked up some brochures describing the Women's Army Corps and decided that joining up just might be a better way to help the war effort than with a riveting gun or a soldering iron in her hand.

"It just couldn't be any harder," she told her friends, "and besides, I would get to travel."

She also convinced several of the single girls at work to enlist, and they marched down to the recruiting station with her. When it came time to sign up, however, a few of them backed out. Several of the girls, including Juanita, did enlist and were sworn in right then and there. Although only 17, Lillie was able to sign up because her friends told her about a guy who could fudge her birth certificate.

Lillie left her job at the plant and was given a farewell party. Some of the girls pooled their money and bought her a watch.

Tears were shed when Lillie, Juanita, and a few other brave girls left the Willow Run defense plant for the last time.

Early in the morning of August 14, 1944, Lillie found herself on her way back "down south," as the girls boarded a train bound for Savannah, Georgia.

After a stop in Richmond, Virginia, to complete more induction paperwork, the train moved on to Georgia. At the Savannah station, several troop trucks were waiting to pick them up. Many young girls from all over America were hopping up into the back of the trucks. It was all very exciting.

Lillie and Juanita were laughing and crying at the same time. "Oh Lil, what have we done?" cried Juanita.

"Don't worry, honey, we're going to be just fine. I may finally meet the man of my dreams down here, and marry me a rich soldier!" said Lillie.

"I don't think that there is any such thing as that!" laughed Juanita.

All of the girls sitting in the back of the truck laughed and carried on all the way to the base.

New Adventures

The young women were driven to the new WAC Training Center at Fort Oglethorpe, Georgia, and issued uniforms.

Private Collins

Lillie felt that hers was a bit too big in some places and was about to start complaining about it when she turned and saw her reflection in the mirror. There, looking back at her was Lillie-Maude Collins, of Roanoke Rapids, North Carolina, all dressed up in the uniform of the United States Women's Army Corps. She wept like a little girl.

She was so proud to be a WAC!

Take that, Kenneth!

Lillie in fatigues

CHAPTER FOUR

LUCKY TO BE ALIVE

In the book *Band of Brothers,* penned by Stephen Ambrose, the author describes a young paratrooper of the 101st Airborne who is flying high over the English Channel on his way to parachute behind enemy lines prior to the invasion of Normandy.

The time is just before dawn. He sits in an open doorway of the transport, resting his back against the doorframe as one leg dangles back and forth in space outside of the plane. The boyish paratrooper gazes about wild eyed at the spectacle that is now playing out all around him.

One hundred planes filled with men like himself from the 101st and the 82nd Airborne are flying in formation. These men will pave the way for the Allied forces of D-day.

The drone of powerful engines fill the cool and damp night air. It has been raining, and nothing can be seen below except cloud cover. Then comes a big break in the clouds, and he can easily make out the channel below. The paratrooper looks down at just the right instant. In that very moment, frozen in time and space, he witnesses a sight that few have ever seen, or will ever see, no matter how long God allows us to breathe the air of this planet.

Below him is the largest armada of war ships ever gathered, steaming toward France. Battleships, destroyers, troop ships, landing crafts of all shapes and sizes, huge vessels of all kinds that have been rebuilt and redesigned to carry all of the equipment and weaponry necessary to put the Allied forces in control of these beaches.

Ships as far as he can see. What a sight this must be for that young paratrooper looking down from that open door. What a sight indeed!

Aboard several of these large ships or LCIs (Landing Craft Infantry) rode G.I. Joe and the Tough Ombres of the 359th Regiment of the 90th Infantry Division. The soldiers were packed in like sardines, making movement next to impossible. Many of the men were seasick, making the experience all the worse.

These men had been aboard these boats for almost three days already. While the rain fell hard and final plans were being hammered out by the high command, most of the first assault teams were cruising in circles just off the English Coast. After that trans-Atlantic trip and now this ordeal, G.I. Joe swore that if he ever made it through this war alive, he would never, under any circumstance whatsoever, climb aboard a boat of any kind, ever again.

And he never did!

While the navy pounded the Normandy beaches with heavy artillery fire, the Tough Ombres were suddenly only several hundred yards from shore. Wearing their T-O patches, they found themselves alongside and now part of the Fourth Infantry who were wearing four-leaf crest patches.

Together, they descended on rope ladders from the bigger LCTs and LCIs into the smaller landing crafts (LCVPs).

Utah Beach, June 6, 1944

There were 30 men to a boat, with one coxswain or driver wearing a flack jacket. He would be the one to pilot the craft into the beach. He would build speed and virtually crash the craft onto the beach as he lowered the big ramp. The men would pile off as one and begin the bloodiest assault of World War II.

Uncle Red

G.I. Joe was now part of a rifle support group for a Beach Obstacle Demolition Party that would hit the beach code-named "Utah." They were part of the first wave of soldiers. They would come ashore somewhere in the vicinity of the landing zone (LZ) that was code-named Uncle Red.

Frightened and still feeling weak and shaky from being seasick, G.I. Joe climbed down the rope ladder

Troops push into the beach.

Finding shelter at Normandy

and settled into the LCVP. Huddled up with 29 other men who were all carrying weapons, explosives, bangalore torpedoes, and flamethrowers, as well as a full pack of gear, he was on his way toward the beach.

The adrenaline level was incredible. They were on their way, and their orders were clear: Protect the men who were attempting to blow up the barricades with rifle fire. Then run like mad to the left and upward and onward to the designated meeting and regrouping points.

Engage and kill the enemy and drive him back! Take over all enemy emplacements and secure the beach at all costs.

Allied intelligence and the sheer ingenuity of high command had done everything possible to fool the

Germans into thinking that this invasion would not happen and, even if it did, it would certainly not take place here.

Many of Nazi Germany's elite and seasoned leaders fell for all or part of this ruse. Adolph Hitler was even thought to be taking a nap at the time. The German army was not as prepared for the assault at Normandy as they could have been.

Tell that to the men who hit the beaches of Normandy, France, code-named Omaha and Utah, on D-day, June 6, 1944. It was the classic case of the movable force coming to grips with the seemingly unmovable object.

The landing at Utah Beach by the Fourth Infantry with elements of the 90th did not meet quite as much resistance as their counterparts at Omaha, but it was certainly no picnic!

While First Infantry, known as the Big Red One, and the 29th were taking on very heavy fire and many casualties at Omaha, the men at Utah also had their hands full with the German army.

Omaha had more obstacles and more fire raining down on them, but Utah beach was more heavily mined. Many of our boys were getting blown to bits as they ran. The problems on both beaches resulted from navy fire-power coming up short and killing many of our own men.

The Germans came with mortar fire and machine guns. Their heavy duty 88s also pounded the beaches with heavy ordnance.

Utah Beach today
(Photo by Steven M. Robinson)

At the End of the Day

The LCVPs dropped the ramp and the men attacked the beach. G.I. Joe ran and fired. He followed orders and provided cover for the demo teams. Men died all around him, and still he ran and fired. Everything was made more difficult by the fact that the landing craft had missed their originally planned LZs — some by as much as 1,500 yards!

None of the plans and rendezvous points that the men had memorized and prepared for were the same. With all of the gunfire raining down and with mines exploding all around them, there was some chaos for sure, but for the most part the officers and soldiers adapted, persevered, and eventually succeeded in spite of the many logistical mistakes that were made.

All G.I. Joe knew to do was his job. This was what he was trained for, and he was giving it his best shot.

At the end of the day, the beach was secured. Landing craft of all kinds were unloading bulldozers, tanks, trucks, heavy artillery, and troops into France through Utah and Omaha Beach.

The door was now open, but the cost was high. Counting the United States Airborne losses as well as those of the Canadians, British, and American soldiers who lost their lives on the beaches, more than 9,000 men died that day to further the cause for freedom!

At the end of that day of all days, G.I. Joe felt lucky to be alive!

CHAPTER FIVE

FLYING COLORS

L illie completed basic training and graduated with flying colors from a course in the repair and maintenance of communications equipment.

There exists a wonderful picture of Lillie's graduating class (see following page). Among the hundred or so WACS in the picture, it is easy to pick out the smiling North Carolina farm girl standing tall and proud in the center of the second row. The picture is dated October 21, 1944, and Private Lillie M. Collins wrote these words on the back: "I knew I could do it! I am sorry this good bunch of girls will be parting ways, but that's the army!"

The entire time that Lillie had been away from Roanoke Rapids, she only received one

Newly graduated WACs — 1944

letter. That was from her brother Tom who was stationed overseas in Italy. She figured that most of her family had forgotten about her so she drifted farther and farther away from them.

Lillie loved the army and everything about it and wrote the following in her memoirs:

> You might think it crazy, but, except for the bad haircut they gave me, I simply loved being in the army. Most of the girls in my outfit were also under age, and it was amazing how well we all behaved. As for me, I was afraid that if I did something wrong, they might find out

my age and throw me out. I was so proud of my uniform and my flag. Our boys were dying every day for our country and when I would hear the national anthem, I would cry for them. I got down on my knees every night and prayed for them, one and all.

Lillie's Family

Her orders were to report to Eglin Air Force Base in Fort Walton Beach, Florida. She was now being assigned to the army air force. In those days, the air force was part of the army and it was not uncommon for personnel to be transferred back and forth between the two service divisions. This was especially true of the women.

Lillie told Juanita, "Well, I'll be doggone, they have gone and put me in the air force!"

Her dear friend, Juanita, was heading for Des Moines, Iowa, and eventually the Pacific Theater of Operations (PTO). After the war, they would slowly lose touch with each other, but Lillie never forgot her dear friend. She always said, "Juanita was the best friend that I ever had in my whole life!"

Lillie had a three-day pass before being shipped from Georgia to Florida, so she decided to go home to Roanoke Rapids for a quick visit. She wanted to see her mother and show her father and brothers how well she had done.

If they were indeed impressed, they didn't show it when Lillie arrived home. But Otley, her mother, certainly did. The old woman hugged her daughter and wept. She prayed out loud, "Dear Jesus, protect my daughter, Dear Jesus, protect my daughter!"

After a brief visit, Lillie once again made her way back across the cotton and cantaloupe fields as she had done as a little girl. This time she did so as a private in the U.S. Army. She walked the several miles into town and boarded a bus back to Fort Oglethorpe.

Like G.I. Joe, the U.S. Army had become her family.

Closer to the Action

This was a pivotal time for women in the armed forces. It was 1944, and most enlisted women were becoming very dissatisfied. The men were doing all the fighting, and many WACs felt they were still doing jobs that they referred to as "girly things," such as filing, typing, and other forms of clerical work.

Heck, we could have done this at home, many of them thought.

In most cases, they were right.

Eventually, changes were made, and WACs began to be earmarked for duty closer to the action.

Many of the girls were taught medical assistance skills and shipped off to the Pacific Theater of Operations (PTO) as well as to various points in Europe (ETO) to help care for the wounded.

Although nursing and medical assisting jobs were important, many WACs still wanted to be more involved on the battlefield. Lillie wanted to go to war as well, but orders sent her to an air base in Florida where she would learn to fix and rebuild communication equipment for all sorts of aircraft. She also worked in the radio room.

Airmen

Lillie was very happy at Eglin, and she dated a few airmen now and then. Although she worked hard at her job, Lillie really enjoyed flying! All sorts of aircraft constantly came through

Lillie — WAC at work

the base for repair, training exercises, and maintenance.

On occasion, the flight crews of B24s and B27s would take her up into the clouds for a ride. They would fly out and over the Gulf of Mexico on maneuvers.

Lillie would look down through the bomb bay doors and laugh out loud. Call it the bravado of youth if you will. This same woman would, later on in life, develop a fear of crossing a bridge in a car. In these days of being stationed at Eglin, however, an 18-year-old WAC named Lillie feared absolutely nothing!

She later wrote, "These guys and girls were the greatest. I loved them all. We worked hard every day and went dancing every night. All the flyboys wanted to dance with me. I was good at it!"

She would have one brush with romance while in Florida. A "flyboy" named Kenny had just returned home from the war with a Dear John letter in his hand. The girl back home had left him while he worked as a bombardier dropping heavy ordnance from a Flying Fortress over Germany.

Lillie felt sorry for him and started to date him. Just as their relationship began to blossom, Kenny and his long-lost girlfriend reconciled, and he flew home to some town in the upper Midwest and married her.

Lillie steamed and stewed over this for months. "My heart was broken again!" she wrote. "The heck with it all!"

She threw herself into her work and quit dating altogether.

Lillie would spend well over a year of her military service right there at Eglin Air Base.

Private First Class

In the spring of 1945, the war with Germany was coming to a close. The Russian army was closing in from the east, and the rest of Allied forces had all but taken over Berlin.

The Allies would win the air war with a lot of help from the 20th fighter wing. They had flown the old P-38 fighter planes over G.I. Joe at Normandy. In the summer of 1944, the switch was made to the famous

American-made P-51 Mustangs. The brave pilots flying these incredible airplanes would eventually help to hammer the German Luftwaffe into defeat over the next year.

It was rumored that, after the war, the 20th air group would eventually make their home at Shaw Air Force Base near Sumter, South Carolina, and there was much preparation to be done. (Actually, the 20th did not get to Shaw until 1947.)

Not long after V-E Day on May 8, 1945, Lillie was transferred. After a well-deserved leave spent mostly in Atlanta, Georgia, she reported for duty at Shaw Air Force Base in July of 1945.

Lillie was back in the Carolinas. This time as a private first class in the Women's Army Air Corps!

St. Louis Vacation

Thankfully, the war was now over in Europe, and Japan would surrender on September 2, 1945 (V-J Day).

Our boys were coming home. At Shaw, Lillie's assignment was clerical work of all kinds, and she wasn't happy about it. First off, she wanted to do more than just file paperwork. (She absolutely refused to learn how to type!) She missed the camaraderie of working closely with flight crews, and it appeared that the 20th wasn't coming to Shaw anyway. Besides that, the very air in South Carolina reminded her of home and the farm.

*Lillie and
her friend
Eunice*

Lillie wanted a transfer and finally received one in January of 1946. Her new orders would send her to Long Island, New York, where she would now be stationed at Mitchel Field in Hempstead.

Before reporting for duty, she was awarded another leave. This time she chose to go to St. Louis, Missouri. It was to be the most westward trip she would make in her entire life.

Lillie rented a cheap room for two weeks and went to movies and shows. The weather was crisp and cool, and the young WAC had a ball. Everywhere she went, people applauded her uniform, and it made her cry with pride.

She made friends with a girl named Eunice who had been discharged from the service a month earlier. She had been a WAC nurse in the Pacific Theater, working on a hospital ship.

Lillie told her new friend about Leonard and more recently Kenny and her close brush with romance in Florida.

Eunice had a few words of advice for her friend, which went something like this: "Whatever happens, Lil, don't get yourself hooked up with no soldier. You're just asking for it if you do!"

Eunice and Lillie wrote back and forth for years after the war.

Battle Scarred

On January 28, 1946, Lillie arrived for duty at Mitchel Field. It was here, in Hempstead, Long Island, where she would come to witness first hand the pain and sacrifice of the men who had fought in combat. She would never forget the experience.

The injuries she saw during this time would haunt Lillie for the rest of her life. Perhaps this experience provided an anchor of sorts for Lillie's understanding, her tolerance beyond measure, unending dedication, and pure unmitigated, constant love for the battle-scarred young soldier that she was soon to marry.

☆

☆

☆

☆

☆

Yes, it would be here at Mitchel Field that she would meet and fall "head over heels in love" with a tough Philadelphia street kid turned infantryman named . . . G.I. Joe!

CHAPTER SIX

THE HEROES THAT DAY

Being among the first Allied troops to step onto French soil, G.I. Joe and the elements of the 359th who were attached to the Fourth Infantry became the first unit of the Fighting 90th to see action. On June 7 and 8, the 357th and 358th regiments would land and come ashore at Utah Beach. At the same time, the 90th Infantry Division began to organize themselves in preparation for moving inland.

On D-day plus three, G.I. Joe was called up before his commanding officer. He was given back his stripe. Private First Class G.I. Joe was awarded the Bronze Star for "valor on the beaches of Normandy."

Years later, he told his son about his experiences. He only told it once.

"I never did anything that everyone else wasn't doing on the beach," he began. "I did my job and helped my buddies when I could. Other than that, I ran like a rabbit.

"Bullets kept passing by my head. I could hear them. Some whistled, and some had more of a buzzing sound.

"Between the mines going off and the constant mortar fire plus all the racket the navy was making, I thought I had gone plumb deaf. My hearing kept fading in and out. Men were dying all around me. Blood and body parts were everywhere. I heard a lot of screaming.

"I just kept running until I made it to a crest in a hill beyond the beach. There, I joined a group of other soldiers.

"We looked back and, through all the smoke, we could see more men coming ashore. The new arrivals had to dance around the dead and dying bodies to make any progress.

"Along with the other fellows, I climbed on over the ridge and began to shoot at the Germans. We killed a lot of them, too!

"Later, they pinned the Bronze on me. I didn't deserve it. They should have pinned it on the dead guys. They were the heroes that day."

Inch by Inch

On June 10, the Tough Ombres were about to move inland as a unit for the first time. The combat that would take place over the next three months would change G.I. Joe forever. Utah Beach was hell enough, but it was a cakewalk compared to the hell that was waiting in the days and weeks ahead.

This paraphrased report from the military archives explains what G.I. Joe and his comrades faced that day:

On June 10, the 90th Infantry Division made its first attack as a division. From the heavy resistance in and around the towns of Picauville, Cauquingy, and Pont l'Abbe to the Mahlman line, the 90th Infantry Division participated in some of the most difficult, demanding, and bloodiest battles of the war.

Before the breakout was complete, they had to survive the deadly "hedgerow" fighting. Another paraphrased report from the military archives noted:

The hedgerows of Normandy were designed by the French to conserve the soil and to prevent erosion, but they also made for ideal lines of defense. You could place a strong force of Wehrmacht defenders in one row and cover the approaches with murderous fire from arms. At each end of a row properly placed machine guns could sweep the fields before them with deadly crossfire.

If somehow the Americans succeeded in neutralizing the defense of row number one, row number two would go into action with deadly mortars zeroed in on the fields. Row number three was well defended with 88s and other artillery of various calibers with all possible targets in range duly noted and accurately plotted.

It was a great strategy, and the German army figured the Americans would lose heart and go back into the sea toward England.

The men of the 90th Division had other plans, and pushed forward inch by inch, with no intention of returning to the sea. Day after day, they lashed out at the Germans with guns, knives, and even their bare fists. It was perhaps the bravest assault on an enemy in the history of modern warfare.

The German plan was indeed a good one, but because of men like G.I. Joe and those fighting beside him wearing the T-O patch, the plan didn't work!

G.I. Joe would never talk about the hedgerows to anyone. Apparently, those distinct battles had a very profound effect on him.

One thing remained constant, every day and throughout most of his nights during this campaign, for this brave G.I.: constant combat on a very primitive level!

Men dying, men wounded, men killing men either from a distance or, as in the case of the hedgerows, up close and personal — hand-to-hand and eye-to-eye.

Men on the front lines were relieved from time to time, but for the most part, the fighting was continuous. In every account that has been written about this battle of the war in Europe, the words "vicious" or "bloody" usually appear before the words "hedgerow battles" or "hedgerow fighting."

Like D-day itself, this was a time of pure hell on earth for many of our American boys, and it should never be forgotten.

Legends in the Making

The men of the 90th Infantry broke out of the Normandy peninsula in August of 1944. They were starting to become renowned all over the military as a crack fighting unit.

Their deeds and accomplishments, as well as their sacrifice on the field of battle, were put forth as examples to be emulated by fresh reinforcements who were arriving every day. Commanding officers, as well as grunts, all along the front lines talked about the 90th as if they had already become legends. A sort of folklore began to build around them.

They were indeed a well-trained and highly disciplined bunch of fighting men who attacked every mission with the highest resolve and efficiency. The more men they lost, the meaner they became. God help the Nazi Kraut who got in their way.

At a place called the Falaise Pocket, G.I. Joe's 359th Infantry Regiment defeated the German 7th Army in a bloody battle that lasted four days.

They captured 13,000 prisoners, killed or wounded over 8,000 soldiers, and destroyed almost 4,000 vehicles, tanks, self-propelled guns, and artillery pieces. In contrast, the 359th suffered less than 600 killed or wounded. Tough Ombres, indeed.

It is interesting to note that the 90th Infantry Division was recommended for the Presidential Unit Citation by General Patton.

In the book *History of the 90th,* the author notes that Patton's recommendation was returned for revision because he could only recommend ten percent of his units for this award. In his revised recommendation, the general reduced the number of units but insisted that the entire 90th Infantry Division receive this award. The 90th Infantry Division is the only division Patton officially recommended for this distinguished award.

Single-handed

After the men of the 90th had been placed under the command of General George S. Patton, G.I. Joe and the 359th Regiment were fighting under the banner of the Third Army.

The critical advancement toward Germany was fast and bloody. Patton's army would march on toward

Fountainbleu and around Paris. At the battles of Reims and Metz, they helped to push the German Siegfried line back, and eventually marched right on up to the paperhangers' doorstep in Berlin.

G.I. Joe, however, would never make it that far. His days of combat were quickly coming to an end. In late July of 1944, on or around D-day plus 50, somewhere on a hillside in France, Private First Class G.I. Joe finally snapped!

With his entire platoon pinned down by two enemy machine gun nests, the barrage of enemy fire was constant. The men were not able to move an inch.

A young lieutenant whom G.I. Joe had become fond of decided to position himself on higher ground in order to get a better assessment of the situation at hand. He was hit almost immediately. So incredibly hard was the impact of the 50-caliber shells that his head was blown off.

As the head rolled back down the hill, it came to a stop right by G.I. Joe. The eyes staring up at him still seemed to possess a small spark of life. Before going blank, they blinked once.

G.I. Joe screamed at the top of his lungs and rose up from his crouched and hidden position. He immediately took several rounds of machine gun fire to his hip and buttock. He started to run toward the enemy. A German grenade and several mortar shells exploded near him, and his body was ravaged with fragmentation.

☆
☆
☆

G.I. Joe kept on running, all the while screaming and shooting and tossing hand grenades of his own. He was then shot in the foot, the leg, and lower back, yet somehow managed to keep on running.

G.I. Joe single-handedly killed every last German soldier who manned those emplacements, and in so doing saved his entire platoon. He was thought to be dead and was, in fact, left lying in his own blood for several days.

Almost four months would pass before G.I. Joe would remember any of what had happened. He woke up one day in an army hospital bed in Saint Lo, France, with a Silver Star and a Purple Heart with two oak leaf clusters pinned to his pillow.

He was just 20 years old.

CHAPTER SEVEN

THE NATION'S WOUNDED

B y the time Lillie arrived in Long Island in 1946, all of America seemed to be celebrating and grieving at the same time. Such was the case at the many base hospitals that were taking on the nation's wounded.

Yes, the war was over, but flag-draped coffins were arriving each day by the planeload. The big C-47 transports kept on bringing the wounded home as well. Although the nation was cheering, it was also the beginning of the healing process. This was a very unique and emotional time in the history of our great land.

Mitchel Field had been a virtual hotbed of activity throughout the entire war. This installation on Long Island was the home of three top-level hospitals that specialized in caring for the physical and mental needs of the many wounded men who were shipped there on a daily basis. Before as well as after the war, tens of thousands of wounded men were shipped from overseas battlefields to Mitchel, where they were cared for and, in many cases, processed on to another medical facility. Many were also discharged from the armed service here in Hempstead.

Mitchel Field was also the home of three massive prisoner of war camps where several thousand German army prisoners had been contained during the last few years of the war.

By the time Lillie arrived, the prisons were being dismantled, and the incoming wounded had become the sole priority of Mitchel Field.

No Hero

G.I. Joe was shipped stateside sometime around the end of February 1945. A U.S. Army Air Force C-47 transport flew him to Fort Hood near Killeen, Texas, where he spent his entire time at the military hospital.

When Germany surrendered to the Allies on the eighth day of May, G.I. Joe celebrated V-E Day with yet another operation to remove shrapnel from his lower back. He had already been operated on several times back in France, as well as earlier at Fort Hood. Joe's body must have been full of the horrible stuff because, over time, it kept on regurgitating those awful pieces of metal.

Army doctors and, later, Veterans Administration surgeons would repeat this procedure over and over again, removing more and more shrapnel from his arms and legs, as well as his complete upper and lower torso. This was a procedure that he would have to tolerate for the rest of his life.

He was released from the hospital in Fort Hood just once in order to attend a medals ceremony where he was to be one of the honorees. Several young soldiers were assigned to help him get to and from the event and would also be there to help him take the stand when his name was called.

However, he simply refused to go with them. He stayed in his bed. "I am no hero. The *heroes* didn't come back!" he told the young soldiers, and he literally ran them off.

For disobeying orders and not showing up, he once again lost that PFC stripe. Being busted back to a private again didn't seem to matter much to G.I. Joe. They could not have dragged him to that ceremony!

Truck Driver

On September 30, 1945, some officers surrounded Joe's bed and handed him his honorable discharge papers. They told him that if he were to go home to Philadelphia he could be put under the care of the naval hospital there. He signed the declaration of separation from the U.S. Army and sat up all night long pondering over his future.

Joe couldn't walk yet, and at that point he was not sure that he ever would. Besides, he suspected that the army felt he was a bit crazy and didn't want him around anymore, which was probably true. Some of Joe's nightmares were so traumatic that his horrifying screams had scared the nurses half to death.

The very next day, October 1, 1945, Joe decided to re-enlist. Since he had no one at home who cared a lick about him anyway, Joe signed up right there in his hospital bed at Fort Hood. He figured that the army was the only place where he would be understood, and they could certainly take much better care of him than his own family ever could or would. On his enlistment papers in the box marked, "field of expertise," G.I. Joe penciled in "truck driver." Considering all that he had been through, he still possessed a rather keen sense of humor.

The army, however, wasn't laughing. It had its hands full of shot-up and beat-up soldiers to care for after V-E Day. By the time the Japanese had surrendered on September 2, 1945 (V-J Day), every military and civilian hospital in the country was being pushed beyond its limits. Thousands of wounded young men were shipped home from overseas day after day, week after week, and month after month.

At the end of March, the army doctors and psychologists at Fort Hood thought that G.I. Joe could be better served somewhere else. On March 26, 1945, he was shipped to the Santini Sub Base, New Cantonment Hospital at Mitchel Field in Hempstead, Long Island, New York.

"All Alone in a Foxhole"

Although it was merely a technicality, Lillie was declared officially out of the air force and back in the army. Her uniform stayed the same. She still loved being a WAC, and her respect for her uniform and the girls who wore it continued to grow.

Lillie later said, "The girls in the army were all great. I loved every one of them and would stick up for any of them with my life. All of the WACs stationed here at Mitchel Field served their country well. The end of the war would have been even harder without these girls. God bless them all."

She was assigned to a processing center where her job was to help expedite the wounded back into the country. It was back to clerical work for Lillie and she hated it. When she heard that some WACs were being selected to fly overseas and help escort the wounded home, she jumped at the chance.

All of a sudden she found herself aboard a C-47 along with several other WACs on a two-day flight to Europe. They would eventually land at bases near London or Paris, load the boys on the plane and bring them back to Mitchel Field.

"I made sure all their paper work was in order, so that they could go home," Lillie said.

After returning to the States, the WACs would rest for a day then climb back aboard a plane bound for Europe, and do it all over again.

On these trips and in the processing center, Lillie saw the horrible result of combat and witnessed first-hand the price paid by the soldiers. Some had lost legs or arms or eyes in the service of their country. It was heartbreaking.

Although the soldiers' physical deformities were heartbreaking to see, the mental cases were just as devastating. Men stared straight ahead with their eyes wide open without seeming to see anything. They were on their way home, but they could not comprehend what that meant. The sight of all these broken young boys was tough for the young WACs to behold.

Lillie threw herself into this job with all of her heart and soul. Aboard the transports, she would spend time with as many soldiers as she could and attempt to comfort them. She would pray for them, talk to them, and even sing to them.

Her repertoire consisted of three Gospel songs: "The Gloryland Way," "Dust on the Bible," and "Jesus on the Mainline."

Another old ballad started with the words, "Last night all alone in a foxhole . . ." but that was as far as she could get. Lillie would look at these men and begin to weep.

For the rest of her life she would attempt to sing that song, but as soon as she would get to the word "foxhole," she would remember those boys coming home and break down. "I could have fallen for all of them," she said later. "I loved them all!"

How About a Kiss?

Lillie landed at Mitchel Field early one morning and, as was her custom, proceeded to her barracks and prepared to climb into her bunk. Before settling in, she received word that the process center was backed up, and they were extremely short-handed. The center was, in reality, merely a converted hanger where the arriving shipment of men waited for the WACs to get all of their paperwork in order. Lillie, of course, was happy to pitch in.

When she walked into the hanger, the usual array of wounded soldiers was everywhere; sitting down, standing up, lying on stretchers, talking, laughing, weeping, and waiting for their paperwork to be completed.

He was sitting in a wheel chair in a corner all alone. The wounded soldier appeared to be in some discomfort. His left leg was encased in some sort of metal cast, and some kind of a brace was visible around his waist. The casual observer could barely make it out under his uniform, but it was there.

From way across the hanger Lillie took notice of the soldier and thought that he might need some attention. She walked toward him. G.I. Joe looked up and saw her coming.

When she got just a bit closer, he winked at her. She smiled at him.

G.I. Joe smiled back and softly said, "Hello, Doll."

"Are you okay, Honey?" she asked.

☆
☆
☆

"Oh yeah, doing just fine. You?"

"Me? Hey, I am doing just peachy."

Oh my, she liked this guy.

"Okay, then, how about a kiss?" said G.I. Joe as he looked up at Lillie.

"And why would I kiss you just like that? Give me a reason."

"Well," he said, without missing a beat. "I've never kissed another soldier before."

Lillie leaned over and kissed G.I. Joe right on the lips. She fell in love with him then and there.

"Head over heels!" Lillie said later. "He was the most handsome man that I had ever seen. Sitting there in that uniform he looked like a movie star. At least to me he did. I fell for him in a heartbeat. I would have married him on the spot."

"Let me see your paperwork, Honey," Lillie said.

G.I. Joe reached into an inside pocket and produced his orders. He was still smiling when he handed them to her.

"You have only been in the army since October?" she asked.

How could this be? thought Lillie. *A truck driver?*

G.I. Joe then handed Lillie his discharge papers.

"I re-enlisted," he whispered.

Lillie scanned his papers: Silver Star, Bronze Star, Purple Heart, Normandy, 359th, 90th, St. Lo, wounded in action.

Oh my, dear God, bless him.

Lillie handed him back his papers. Her eyes were full of tears. She leaned over, took him in her arms, and kissed him again. This time on the forehead. Lillie then stood back up and looked deeply into his eyes. She loved what she saw there.

"I'll take you on over to the Santini Sub Base," she said and began to wheel him out of the process center toward the New Cantonment Hospital.

The very next day G.I. Joe asked an army chaplain named Jack Moses, "How can I get a marriage license?"

CHAPTER EIGHT

HEAD OVER HEELS

L ove at first sight was something Lillie never thought would happen to her. Since she had been jilted a few times already, her radar was up and running when it came to men.

One explanation for her "head-over-heels" condition could have been the shear pain of seeing all of these broken young men returning stateside day after day into Hempstead. She said many times that she loved them all, and I believe she did.

Perhaps seeing G.I. Joe opened up all of Lillie's pent-up emotions. In him, she may have seen them all, and on some level attached herself to the many, through him.

He was needy, and she was more than willing to fill the need. Whatever the case, it was indeed "love at first sight." She liked him right off. He stirred her heart when he looked up and said those first words to her.

From G.I. Joe's standpoint, he had never thought much about romance at all. He certainly liked the girls, but he never had a childhood sweetheart of any kind. Lately, well, he had been kind of busy.

The answer to their instant attachment to one another is really very easy to explain. God meant for these two to meet, fall in love, and marry. It is as simple as that.

From the beginning the two were destined to be together. So raise the flag and strike up the band — G.I. Joe and Lillie are getting married!

The Big Event

Before the wedding, Lillie had a long talk with her CO.

"These kind of relationships are emotional and never last," the officer warned.

"In my heart I knew that I loved this man," Lillie said later, "so I married him anyway."

The United States Army went all out for G.I. Joe and Lillie's wedding. They provided flowers and decorations as well as a nice cake. Although small by wedding standards, it was a big event for the army.

On the base was a large Lutheran church. After counsel with the chaplain, the aforementioned Jack Moses, the young soldiers were both christened into the Lutheran faith.

Happy wedding party

That was just fine with G.I. Joe because he had never been christened as anything. As for Lillie, she believed that Jesus Christ was her Savior who lived in her heart, and that was all that really mattered.

In Roanoke Rapids, North Carolina, there were only Baptists and Methodists. In reality, Lillie didn't know what a Lutheran was.

Chaplain Moses had signed their license to marry on March 27, just one day after G.I. Joe arrived at Mitchel Field. Six days later, on the afternoon of April 2, 1946, he presided over the wedding and, before cheering soldiers, airmen, and WACs, he pronounced

Cutting the cake!

G.I. Joe and Lillie "Man and wife. To have and to hold in sickness and health."

"The full military wedding was beautiful," Lillie said later, "and the post commander gave me away. My friends in the WACs gave us a large reception after the ceremony."

"All I have to give you, Lillie," Joe had told his fiancée, "is my love."

He was right! Joe didn't have a cent and sold his watch to buy Lillie's ring. Fortunately the newlyweds received $600 in gifts that would come in handy later.

The Santini Sub Base hospital had provided G.I. Joe with a special leg brace and cane so he could stand up for the wedding. It was underneath his pants and not visible in the wedding pictures. It was a happy day for both of them.

Two people who thought that they "had nobody" now had each other.

Lillie pledged to her God, "I will be a good wife to this young soldier — steadfast and true through thick and thin."

The years ahead would provide a lot of thin, but Lillie would keep her promise to God and to G.I. Joe.

They consummated their marriage in a small cottage provided by the base for one night only. After the short honeymoon, it was back to the hospital for G.I. Joe and back to the process center for Lillie.

Lillie ended her army career as a clerical worker and never flew overseas again. She had a husband now, and he came first.

Nightmares

Over the next six months, G.I. Joe showed remarkable improvement. The hours of rehabilitation on his shot-up legs and feet began to pay off. His back also began to feel better as the wounds started to heal, and he was able to walk fairly well.

The nightmares, however, were still a serious issue. His dark dreams of combat and death were a real and constant problem.

Some men who fought the war could seemingly forget the experience, or at least push it far enough back into the recesses of their minds so as not to focus on the subject for very long. If a soldier expects to come home from war and lead any kind of normal life, it is imperative to deal with the trauma of battle.

No one can ever completely forget the hell of combat as it occurred on D-day and in the days following. It is always there, like that aforementioned piece of luggage.

Every human being is different and so are the mental capabilities of each person to be able to deal with what is called in this day and age, Post-war Syndrome or Post-traumatic Stress Syndrome.

Long before these catch phrases came into vogue, veterans were plagued by nightmares that made it all but impossible to live a normal life. Probably every man or woman who has experienced combat in any war has suffered from various mental problems on many different levels. There is no way around it.

Seeing your friends blown to bits before your eyes is a life-changing experience for any soldier involved in wartime conflict and has been so since the first wars and right up to today.

Modern medicine and psychological approaches to healing the trauma are more advanced now, and many veterans who served in Vietnam and the Gulf War, as well as the war on terrorism have benefited from the help available. Still, the many problems outnumber any cure.

For G.I. Joe and many other men who arrived back in the United States from the Pacific and the European campaigns, the experience of war would never leave them. Only the dead were spared the nightmares.

Preparing for Civilian Life

For many of these men, the battle trauma affected every aspect of their lives as well as the lives of their loved ones. Although they certainly tried, the military was hard pressed to help them.

While G.I. Joe made headway at Santini, Lillie took a job as cashier at a movie theater.

"We knew we would never make it on what the army paid us," Lillie explained, "so I got a job to help make ends meet. It was hard serving at my army job all day and working at night at the movies, but I wanted us to have a little money saved up for when we got out of the service."

Her hard work in the army earned her another promotion in the summer of 1946, when she was promoted to corporal. Corporal Lillie liked to remind G.I. Joe that he was outranked.

Eight months after the wedding, on December 17, 1946, the army did a nice thing for G.I. Joe and Lillie. They became the first married couple to be discharged together from Mitchel Field.

G.I. Joe had spent three years and six months in the service of his country, and Lillie had been a WAC for two years, three months and 12 days. Before they were sent back into civilian life, the couple received Good Conduct Medals and American Theater Medals, as well as a World War II Victory Medal.

First they went to New York City and celebrated for three days. "We had a real honeymoon," according to Lillie. "It was wonderful, and we bought some clothes."

Their tentative plan was to consider moving to Philadelphia and buying a home there. G.I. Joe was given a job recommendation letter signed by Major Charles Webb Jr., as well as all the necessary paperwork that would enable him to report to the Philadelphia Naval Hospital for further treatment.

The letter from Major Webb read, in part, "Any man who has the courage and ability to do what this man did on that day in July of 1944, certainly is more than deserving of a chance (to be given him if possible by YOU, Mr. Citizen) to make good at home."

When G.I. Joe and Lillie arrived in Philadelphia, they had nowhere to go. After taking their financial situation into account, they realized that their choices were few. They rented a cheap hotel room downtown near the Thirtieth Street train station and weighed their options.

"We could always just go to North Carolina," Lillie suggested.

"Nah, no good."

"I could call my friend Eunice in St Louis. Maybe she can come up with something. Or we could go to Detroit. I know that town pretty well," Lillie said softly while sitting cross-legged on the edge of the bed.

"No, uh-uh," G.I. Joe muttered as he looked out of a window that faced the City Hall building at Broad and Market Streets.

G.I. Joe liked Philly just fine. He knew these streets well and felt like he and Lillie could do just as well living right here as anywhere else.

He turned from the window and shared his heart with his wife, "Let's stick to the plan. Stay right here, in Philadelphia!"

Lillie thought about this suggestion for a while. *Philadelphia is so big and loud, but the Naval Hospital is here. If that is what he wants to do. . . .*

"All right! That sounds okay, but what do we do next?" Lillie asked. "We don't have a lot of money left, Honey."

G.I. Joe decided that, until he could get a good job and save up some money for a down payment on a house, they would move in with his family on Trenton Street!

Lillie was about to experience combat.

CHAPTER NINE

ANGELS AT THE CROSSROADS

W hy in the world did you marry her? A fat southern girl! That's just great! Weren't the girls around here good enough for you? Is this what the army did for you?" Eleanor ranted on and on from the moment G.I. Joe and Lillie stepped inside the train house on Trenton Street.

Lillie was already a bit apprehensive, and her insides turned over the minute they got out of the cab. G.I. Joe had tried to prepare her for the home of his childhood, but this place was awful. She was feeling more sorry for her husband by the minute.

He grew up here?

To make matters worse, the insults of her new mother-in-law hurt Lillie deeply. In fact, she never recovered from that first encounter. She didn't like this woman at all, and she never would.

Their stressful living conditions did not improve over the next few months. Lillie's in-laws seemed incapable of co-existing as human beings, and sleeping in that house night after night was taking an emotional toll on the newlyweds.

To make matters worse, when G.I. Joe went to the Philadelphia Naval Hospital for a checkup and evaluation, they immediately admitted him for observation and surgery. He would be there for five months as more shrapnel was removed from his body.

Lillie was devastated.

"I felt so all alone," she remembered. "I got a job working in the J.R. Berry and Sons furniture store and also learned how to take the city bus to the Naval Hospital to see Joe. I went there every other day.

"I cried myself to sleep every night. His mother was simply awful, and she was the best of the lot. I knew one thing for certain. I could not stay in that house any longer. I had to do something.

"When I told my mother-in-law that I would be moving out, she really told me off. We had another big fight. I grabbed up my things and walked out. Even the cab driver felt sorry for me."

Lillie left the train house on Trenton Street on or about February 1, 1947. She took on a full-time job at the Felins Meat Packing House and rented a small room for herself in a boarding home. With Joe in the hospital, she was determined to work hard and provide for him because, "He fought the war, and he came first!"

She prayed every night, "Lord, bless me with something good."

The Crossroads Theory

I have a theory. I call it "The Crossroads Theory."

I believe that everyone comes to several very profound or important crossroads on their journey through life. I also believe that God, in His infinite wisdom, places certain people at those crossroads.

If our minds and hearts are open enough to God's plan and we are willing to listen to His still small voice of guidance, then our eyes will be opened. We will find a special person or two who will influence our decisions as to whether or not to turn right or left. This guidance can change and influence the course of our lives.

In June of 1947 Lillie found herself at such a crossroad. She was very depressed. She was working hard every day and taking long rides on the bus to visit her husband. At the same time, she began looking for a second job.

In an effort to save money, Lillie hardly ate anything. As a result, her own health was starting to suffer. She had just turned 22 years old in January and felt as if the weight of the world was on her shoulders. And it was.

Then, God blessed her with something good!

Angel in a Business Suit

Mr. Theodore Gruenbaum, a businessman who was well into his sixties, stood about six feet, four inches and weighed over 250 pounds. He sold huge machines to the Felins Meat Packing House.

One day, right out of the blue, he stopped and spoke to Lillie. "Mr. Felins himself thinks the world of you," he told the young woman. "He says that you are the hardest worker he has ever seen, so I convinced him to give you a raise."

With that he put his hands on his rather massive belly and laughed out loud. Lillie really liked this man right away.

As they stood and talked for a long time, Lillie shared her story about G.I. Joe and her life in the army.

Mr. Gruenbaum knew he liked this young woman very much. Her dedication and work ethic as well as her service to the country greatly impressed him.

Later, Lillie learned that Mr. Gruenbaum lost two brothers and a sister in a Nazi death camp.

"Here is my address and phone number," he said. "Someday I would love to have you to our home for dinner. Mrs. Gruenbaum makes the best stew that you have ever tasted. Call me sometime."

Lillie took him up on his invitation and visited the Gruenbaum home, which was located in the wealthy section of Philly called City Line. This meant taking a bus from downtown Philadelphia to the city suburbs,

but Lillie was determined to conquer her fears. Before long, she was familiar with all of the bus routes of the PTC (Philadelphia Transportation Corporation).

Lillie fell in love with Mr. and Mrs. Gruenbaum.

"They were angels sent to me by God — the finest two people I would meet in my whole life," Lillie said later. "She was a wonderful woman whom I loved immediately, and he was a big man that I would have trusted with my life."

"I would really like to buy a house," Lillie told Mr. Gruenbaum. "In fact, I have saved a little over $1,800."

"That's wonderful," he said. "I sell real estate, and I know of a house that is for sale."

He paused for a moment and then continued, "In fact, I think I can get you that place for about that amount."

The next day, Mr. Gruenbaum phoned Lillie and told her to meet him at 2119 North Fifth Street.

Although it was a very small row house in the middle of the block, Lillie felt that it would be a good place to start a home.

"It took all the money I had saved," Lillie remembered. "I also had to sign a small note with the bank. Mr. Gruenbaum paid for all of the closing costs. I knew that if I continued to work two jobs, I could manage the payments even if my husband wasn't able to work for a while."

Lillie quit her job at the Berry Furniture store and took a higher paying part-time job at the Frankoweave Textile Corporation. She was so happy. With the extra money, Lillie was able to purchase a mattress for the living room floor, two lamps, a small refrigerator, and a hot plate to "make soup." She lived there by herself, working at Felins in the day and at Frankoweave at night.

Home at Last

Whenever possible, Lillie went to visit G.I. Joe, but she didn't tell him about the house until she brought him home from the Naval Hospital on August 16, 1947.

When that special day came, Lillie took Joe to the house on Fifth Street. He cried when he saw it.

By the time Joe arrived, Lillie had purchased a living room couch from J.R. Berry and Sons, where she had worked while living at the train house. G.I. Joe sat on that couch and continued to weep.

Then she told him all about the Gruenbaums and her two jobs.

"I can't believe you accomplished all this on your own," Joe told his young wife. "I love you so much."

"It's so good to have you home," Lillie said as they nestled together on the new sofa.

"Now it's my turn to get a job," Joe told her. "You've looked after everything, and now it's time for me to pull my own weight."

G.I. Joe was feeling pretty good, and his legs, feet, and back seemed fine. Although the nightmares were still a problem, the navy doctors told him that, in time, they would diminish.

That night G.I. Joe and Lillie made love on the floor of their own home at 2119 North Fifth Street,

Lillie at the house on Fifth Street.

and in almost nine months to the day, on May 18, 1948, their son Joey was born.

A New Addition

Born by caesarean, Joey came out yellow.

That night at the Women's Medical Hospital in downtown Philadelphia, 18 babies were born — 17 were black and one had yellow jaundice.

G.I. Joe rushed to the hospital from his job as a maintenance man at the Yale and Town Corporation. When he ran into the maternity ward and took one look at the baby they told him was his son, he nearly fainted dead away.

Besides the jaundice, the kid was asthmatic. Lillie was also very ill from the childbirth and from just being "so darned run down!"

G.I. Joe was a good soldier though. He managed to guide the family ship through this troubled water, while praying constantly that his son would whiten up, which he eventually did.

Over the next two years, G.I. Joe and Lillie worked very hard. The hospital bills from the rugged birth of their son,

G.I. Joe at the house on Fifth Street

operations on Lillie to repair the childbirth damage, and an unexpected gall bladder removal had to be paid. Added to that were their living expenses and the mortgage payment, but the young couple persevered and even managed to put a few dollars into a savings account.

Mr. Gruenbaum offered to help out, but G.I. Joe and Lillie figured that he had done enough. Besides, their pride dictated that they take care of bills themselves.

Angel at the Door

In order for Lillie to continue working two jobs, she was going to need some help raising baby Joey.

That was when God placed another angel on the crossroad.

Lillie placed an ad in the paper, and it was answered by a wonderful woman by the name of Gertrude Clark.

"I answered the knock at the door, and there she stood. I knew in my heart that God had sent her to us," Lillie noted later.

Nana Clark moved in to the house on Fifth Street and lived in the upstairs back bedroom. Lillie bought a rollaway bed from Berry and Sons for her. Nana's job was to watch Joey and help out with the cooking while G.I. Joe and Lillie worked. By this time, they had also purchased a gas range.

In the spring of 1950, G.I. Joe and Lillie moved. They left their little house on Fifth Street for a larger row house at 3517 Jasper Street by Harrowgate Square

in the Kensington section of North Philadelphia. G.I.
Joe worked out the financing with help from a G.I. loan
and a friendly banker, courtesy of Mr. Gruenbaum.

G.I. Joe proudly carried his wife and his two-year-
old son over the threshold. The house had two stories,
with an enclosed front porch, a living room, dining
room, kitchen, three small bedrooms, and a bathroom
upstairs. Although the house had a very small back-
yard, it had a shed for storage.

G.I. Joe and Lillie in Atlantic City, 1950

Warmth in the winter was provided by a huge coal heater in the cellar. Weekly, a truck would extend a chute through the basement window and drop a load of hard black coal down into a bin in the basement. It was a jarring sound to be sure.

On one side was an alley and on the other side a common wall that was shared with the Brown family next door. That is what makes living in a row house unique. Your wall was someone else's wall as well. G.I. Joe and Lillie would get to know as much about Tom and Peggy Brown and their daughters as they knew about G.I. Joe and Lillie.

Nana Clark didn't move into the house on Jasper Street right away. Instead, she decided to live with her son Cameron and his family in West Philly. Nana commuted to Jasper Street by taking the elevated train to the Tioga Street station, which was just one block away from 3517 Jasper. When the train ran above ground, it was called the el, and, when it dipped below Market Street downtown, it was known as the subway. Thankfully, Nana still continued to look after Joey and the house during the day while G.I. Joe and Lillie made a living.

Going Home

Right about this same time, in the summer of 1950, Lillie received word from her brother Sydney that her mother was failing fast. Lillie took a train to Roanoke Rapids, North Carolina, to visit her. Much like G.I. Joe,

Lillie and Joey

she adored her sweet mother more than anyone else in her family back home. "My father and brothers and even my sister Blanche didn't seem to care if I was there or not," Lillie remembered, "but my sweet Mama sure did."

"I am so proud of you," she told Lillie, "and I love you very much."

Lillie told her all about her husband and son and about being in the army.

"I dearly loved my mother," Lillie said, "I was so glad to have spent some time with her before God called her home."

Jasper Street

Jasper Street in the fifties was a great place to live. All of the neighbors got along well together. The men worked in factories, drove trucks, or were policemen or firemen. Many of G.I. Joe and Lillie's friends had also served in the military, and there was a feeling of camaraderie among most of them.

They often got together to play cards, go to ball games, or go to the Jersey shore to deep-sea fish or walk on the boardwalks. They called it "da shore" as in, "Hey, Lillie, let's drive on down to da shore this Saturday."

While not all the women on Jasper Street were June Cleavers, most were very dedicated to their husbands and worked just as hard as the men to earn a living and raise a family.

The streets were alive with horses and wagons. The voice of the hucksters would ring out each morning,

"Stttrawwwberrieeess, stttrawwwberrieeess." Added to the vendors was the constant sound of trolley cars, buses, and el trains. The streets possessed an incredible and constant energy.

For the most part, these were good times for G.I. Joe and Lillie. Lillie's health was good, and G.I. Joe was working hard. Little Joey was sick most of the time with bronchitis and asthma and spent a lot of time in and out of the hospital, but Nana Clark was always on hand to look after him.

The only dark cloud in their lives was the emotional pain of the reoccurring nightmares that continued to remind the household of the price paid on the battlefields of France. G.I. Joe often woke up screaming and running down the hallway firing imaginary weapons. Lillie often ran after him and gently helped him to wake up. Then she held him in her arms and rocked him like a baby.

From 1947 to 1952, G.I. Joe was an outpatient at the Naval Hospital where he was treated for psychological problems as a result of the war trauma he suffered. He also had several more operations to remove shrapnel.

Following Her Heart

The pressure started to get to G.I. Joe, and he began to drink heavily. He would sometimes go to a bar after work and slug down boilermakers. He started to remind himself of his father. After he lost his job at

Yale and Town, he started working at Crown Can Manufacturing. Lillie stood by his side during this time, but it was very difficult for her. Still, she continued to follow her heart every day.

One has to wonder why she turned out the way she did. What was it that made her so special? She believed that being a good mother was something that God expected of her. Lillie possessed a tremendous pride in all that she did and believed that God would reward her for her perseverance.

Many of us never find true meaning for our lives. We drift around wondering what it is that God wants us to do or not to do. He certainly does not want us to be ignorant of His will for our lives. The Bible says: ". . . be ye not unwise, but understanding what the will of the Lord is." We're also told, "Seek the Lord while he may be found. . . ." Lillie must have understood the wisdom behind this early because she was always sure of herself and never doubted that she was in the center of God's will for her life.

"I went to church every Sunday, and I prayed to my God every night. He never let me down. I hated drinking, but I knew that the war played a big part in my husband's problems. Many of the boys came home from overseas with booze problems, but I made up my mind that I would get Joe through all of this. He was a good man, and I loved him with all of my heart. With God's help, I knew we would be just fine."

Lillie at the house on Jasper Street

A Potpourri of People

On August 24, 1953, Lillie gave birth to a beautiful daughter. They named her after the Frank Sinatra song, "Nancy with the Laughing Face."

When G.I. Joe saw Nancy for the first time, he vowed to Lillie and to God that he would do better, and he did.

With two children to raise, G.I. Joe and Lillie rented out their back bedroom, and a virtual potpourri of people moved through the house on Jasper Street.

There was a Czechoslovakian couple who had escaped from behind the Iron Curtain and a German woman named Emma who fought the war with G.I. Joe every night at dinner. It was a good thing for her that he didn't own an anti-tank gun anymore. He eventually "kicked the Nazi out of the house for good."

In 1955, Nana Clark moved back in with the family and took up residence in that back room. She decided that she would rather live with G.I. Joe, Lillie, Joey, and Nancy than in West Philadelphia. Besides, she was getting older, and the commute was a long one.

On rare occasions, G.I. Joe would take the kids and Lillie to visit his childhood home on Trenton Street. Joey and Nancy thought it to be a cold, creepy, foul place.

Nana Gertrude Clark with Lillie, G.I. Joe, Nancy and Joey

Joe's brother Roy and his wife and two kids had moved in around 1957. The entire family would eventually move from the train house on Trenton Street to a row house on Wakeling Street.

Visiting there, however, was just as weird. It was nightmarish for G.I. Joe's two small children to see Roy drunk on the couch, Grandpa Roy drunk in the kitchen, Grandma Eleanor asleep on the couch with her head laid back and her mouth wide open, and Great Grandma Longstreth constantly hollering and screeching as she lay dying in a huge bed which now occupied the downstairs dining room.

Coming and Going

On through the fifties and into the early sixties, Joey and Nancy and their parents, G.I. Joe and Lillie, sailed their little ship through life. Although they never had a lot of money, they never wanted for much, either.

Lillie and Nancy

There was always food on the table and clothes on their backs.

G.I. Joe took his son to see the Phillies play baseball and the Eagles play football. Lillie still worked at Felins Meat Packing House and, eventually, G.I. Joe would work at the Tastykake Baking Company. From their jobs, they brought home lots of free hot dogs, scrapple, and Tastykakes. G.I. Joe and Lillie made sure that Christmas morning looked as magical as Disneyland.

G.I. Joe's drinking would get out of hand once in a while, and the nightmares continued, but Lillie was always right there to reel him back in when he began to drift back into darker waters.

Nancy was becoming a beautiful young lady, and Joey seemed to be overcoming his asthma problems.

Nancy with her doll, Patty

Kenneth and Otley Collins

Roy Sr. and Eleanor Bonsall

This was also a time of many losses. Kenneth Collins and Roy Sr. passed away, as did two of Lillie's brothers.

Mr. and Mrs. Gruenbaum both died in the same year, 1959. Lillie grieved for weeks over this loss. "They were the best friends that I ever had."

Nana Gertrude Clark passed away in 1961. Cancer took her. "She was the most wonderful woman that I have ever known," wrote Lillie. "I can't imagine what our lives would have been without her."

Joey was especially devastated over the loss of Nana Clark. He and his mom would never forget this angel sent from heaven.

Good Times and Rocky Roads

Lillie and the kids attended the Calvary Church of the Brethren on Venango Street, and even G.I. Joe would go on a rare occasion.

Joey's adolescent years were a real challenge, but, thanks to the youth group at the Calvary Church, he found good Christian kids who took him to see Gospel quartets. Along with Elvis, American Bandstand, and do-wop groups, he grew to love Gospel music.

It was during this time of adolescence and "sorting out" his life that something happened to Joey that would change him forever. In fact, it is the most important event in any person's life because it not only affects the way they will live their life, but also the way they will spend eternity. Joey accepted Christ as his personal Savior, and his mother was very proud of him.

In the summer of 1964, Joey was getting ready to tour Scandinavia with his Frankford High School choir. Little sister Nancy was preparing to enter the unsure adolescent world of the John Paul Jones Junior High. She was becoming more beautiful by the moment.

G.I. Joe had now been employed at American Steel Engineering Corporation for the past five years. He had become a chief electrician and was making a good living for his family.

Several years earlier, Lillie had quit her job at Felins and was now spending all of her time doing church work and "raising my kids." They were the typical middle-class family with lots of good times and rocky roads. They would go to "da shore" in Wildwood or Atlantic City, or picnic and swim at Cedar Lakes in Jersey. They rode the roller coasters at Willow Grove Park in the suburbs and fished and picnicked at Pennypack Park Creek.

The proverbial breadwinner, G.I. Joe went to the factory every day and came home every night. He soaked his feet in Epsom salt, ate Lillie's dinner, watched some TV, and went to bed early. Then, the next day, he would do it all over again.

For the most part, they were living the normal American life — the kind of life that guys like G.I. Joe fought and sacrificed and died for overseas. A big change, however, was coming.

World War II was about to pay G.I. Joe another visit!

Chapter Ten

Love and War

G. I. Joe only talked to his son about the war on one occasion. Joey had badgered and cajoled and begged for days. He was relentless. He just had to know how his daddy won those medals that were shut up in an upstairs bedroom drawer, tucked inside their blue cases and carefully hidden away underneath his father's socks. Lillie had shown them to her son on several occasions and the boy just wanted to know the real story behind the honors.

"Lillie, come in here and sit with me while I talk to this kid. I need you here by my side," said G.I. Joe one night after work.

Lillie took a seat on the chair facing the sofa. G.I. Joe sat next to his son and began to talk. He skimmed over D-day and the Bronze Star and only shared some bits and pieces about that day in July when he was wounded and took out the machine gun nests.

G.I. Joe's eyes filled with tears, and his heart overflowed with love for his young son. He thought about the war and the scars that it had branded upon his very soul.

G.I. Joe then placed his arm around his son's shoulders, pulled him in close, and said some things that Joey would never forget. "I was no hero, Boy. Those medals don't mean a thing. I came back! The real heroes didn't.

"They want you when you're young, Son, because you are stupid. An older man would know better than to be in that hellish situation. I didn't do anything special, I was just mad as hell!"

What Joe said next would haunt his son for years to come.

"There will be another war, Joey," he said sadly, "because there always is. But I promise you, Son, you will never see that hell. They'll take me first, or they will have to fight me to the death, but I promise that you will never go. As God is my witness, they will never take you."

G.I. Joe would keep that promise.

With All My Heart

One summer morning in late July of 1964, Lillie prepared two tuna sandwiches and one peanut butter and jelly and put them inside G.I. Joe's lunchbox. She gently placed an apple inside, closed the lid and snapped the clasp shut. Then, she filled his favorite thermos with Maxwell House coffee. After adding a bit of cream and a few spoonfuls of sugar she screwed the lid on tight.

G.I. Joe came downstairs in his dark blue work clothes, grabbed a piece of toast, and kissed her on the cheek. He picked up his lunchbox and thermos and walked outside to his brand new, used 1959 Ford station wagon.

He threw his tool pouch in the backseat and placed his lunchbox and coffee on the floor by the passenger side. He got behind the wheel and turned the ignition key.

Lillie waved from the doorway as she did every morning. She was quite shocked, however, when her husband got out of the car and slowly walked back toward the house. He took her into his arms and held onto her for several moments.

"Well, this is really something. Are you okay, Honey?" she asked.

He then kissed her full on the mouth and backed away a bit and stared very deeply into her eyes.

"Lillie, I haven't always been the best father and husband, and for that I am very sorry," said G.I. Joe. "I just want you to know that I regret a lot of things. I also wanted you to know that I love you very much."

Tears were falling down both cheeks as he spoke.

"Honey, I know that you love me. You have been a wonderful husband, and the kids love you dearly," she answered.

"Some of the drinking got way out of hand, Lil. I am so sorry for all of that. I have always wanted to do what is right by you and Joey and Nancy," he said while looking down at the front steps.

"God knows that, too, Honey, and He always got us through. I have no complaints Joe, you are a good man," whispered Lillie.

He walked back to the car and turned back to face her one more time before he opened the door.

"I love you, Lillie."

"And I love you, Joe, with all of my heart."

Lillie was a bit apprehensive at this point since the entire scenario was a new experience. He normally kissed her, said goodbye, and drove off to work.

Still he hesitated to leave.

"Hey, handsome soldier, you aren't leaving me are you?" Lillie asked.

"I'll never leave you, Doll, not ever. See ya."

He got into the car, pulled out of the narrow parking space and turned and waved at her one more time. He eased to a stop at the corner, looked both ways and then turned left on to Tioga Street. Lillie stood there on the porch for a while, staring at the empty parking space and then went back inside the house.

Life Interrupted

That morning Joey went off to work at his summer job, and Nancy was around the corner playing with her best friend, Laurie Trout.

Lillie sat back on the sofa and turned on the TV. It was time to watch "her story."

She thought of Nana Clark because they both dearly loved their soap operas. In the early years, when Lillie was at work, Nana would always catch her up on who did what and to whom in that day's "stories."

G.I. Joe always made fun of both of them.

Lillie's thoughts were interrupted by the ringing of the telephone. A deep and dark dread seemed to creep up the middle of her back and she was afraid to answer. She knew that something was wrong. She was right!

"We just found Joe slumped over the machine he had been working on. He is unconscious. It may have been an electrical accident, but at this point, no one knows for certain."

Evelyn Downs walked down Jasper Street, picked up Nancy, and took the child to her house. Evelyn was Lillie's best friend, and the kids called her Aunt Ev.

Aunt Ev explained to Nancy that her father had been hurt at work and that she was to come home with her.

Then Aunt Ev called Joey. He was working at Dr. Frederick R. Rude's small animal hospital on Frankford Avenue. Someday, he hoped to be a veterinarian.

"What hospital?" asked Joey.

"Women's Medical on Lehigh Avenue," answered Evelyn. Her voice was shaking. "Your mother is with him."

"I'm on my way!"

Dr. Rude closed the office and drove the frightened 16-year-old son of G.I. Joe to the hospital.

When Joey first saw his unconscious father, the first thing he did was look at his dad's ankle. There had been a hard lump there that felt like a piece of metal.

Joey had often urged his father to go to the neighborhood doctor and see about it, but G.I. Joe had said that he "was sick and tired of doctors." He refused to get it checked out. The lump had been there for several months and, now, it was suddenly gone!

Joey tried to tell the doctors about the lump, but no one wanted to listen to a kid who had just turned 16 and wore his hair in a huge Elvis pompadour.

Lillie listened to him, though. She always did.

Eventually the doctors told Lillie, "Your husband has had a stroke. There was a clot or an obstruction of some sort that had lodged in a main artery, cutting off the blood supply to his brain. The damage could be permanent. He could be paralyzed for life, if he lives at all."

Joey always believed that it was a piece of shrapnel that started in his foot and eventually floated up to his brain, and it probably was.

"God knows that awful stuff came out of him for his entire life," Joey said later. He cried and cried for his father.

G.I. Joe lay paralyzed in a semi-coma. He would turn 39 in just two days on July 31, 1964.

Once again, it was time for Lillie to shine and, as usual, she would shine brighter than the sun!

I got down on my knees and I asked my God to help me through this. It was the worst thing that could have happened. I had a mortgage hanging over my head and two kids to think about. Nana Clark and the Gruenbaums and even my mother were gone. I sure couldn't count on his side of the family because they just didn't seem to care about anything. I knew I had to make some changes and make them quick. I would have to go back to work.

The doctors called and said again that my husband may not survive this stroke and if he did, he would surely be paralyzed for the rest of his life. Oh dear, sweet Jesus, help me.

Getting Back Together

The Frankford High School a cappella choir was about to embark on a one-month, goodwill tour of Norway, Sweden, and Denmark. The choir, known as the Ambassadors of Song, under the direction of Robert G. Hamilton, had been named the Finest Choir in

America at the Music Educators National Convention in Atlantic City.

The kids raised their own money for the trip by performing benefit concerts all over the Northeast. They also collected S&H Green Stamps, and sold candy and magazine subscriptions. Joey had raised more money than any other kid in the choir, but he wanted to stay home with his mother. Lillie insisted that he take the trip. "I actually wanted him to go overseas with that choir so I could sort things out. He cried, and I cried, but I made him go. I sent Nancy to Aunt Evelyn's house to live for a while. I had to be alone."

Lillie secured two jobs. A full-time job at the Craft-ex Manufacturing Company on Venango Street just two blocks from home and a job working part time, four nights a week at the HL Green Department Store on Frankford Avenue. It was just a short ride on the Frankford el to Green's. She was, all of a sudden, a floor lady and a sales lady at the same time. No more daytime "stories" for a while.

Soon it was September. Joey came home from Scandinavia and told his mother that he would help out all he could. He would work everyday after school at the veterinarian's and on Saturday and Sunday he would become a short-order cook at Bette's Luncheonette on Ontario Street.

"I came home from work one day," Lillie explained, "and there was my little daughter Nancy waiting for me on the front steps. She had been living at Evelyn's for several weeks."

"It's almost time to start school," Nancy said. "I wanted to know if you are going to give me away."

"I fell on my knees and held her to my chest. I cried and cried.

"Go down to Evelyn's and get your clothes," Lillie told her. "You can come home now."

That night Lillie and her two kids slept together in the same bed. They were so happy to be back together.

The next day, they formulated a plan. Joey would take Nancy to school and pick her up when he could. When she was alone, neighbors would look in on her. Joey would help her with homework when he got home from school or work. Then he would put her to bed. Joey and Nancy were to stay in the house and try to behave themselves.

"Times were hard, but I never had any trouble from either one of them. They were good kids," remembered Lillie.

In October, the neighbors threw a block party for Lillie. They closed off the street, hired a band, put up circus games, held raffles, and took donations.

The Browns, the Wiechetals, the Fussmans, the Kanes, the Trouts, and the Downs families threw in all the money that they could spare to help G.I. Joe and Lillie.

It was a fun night with pony rides, and a merry-go-round. Joey sang a few Elvis songs with the band.

Lillie sang "Gloryland Way" with the Calvary Church choir.

Reverend Elwin Kirchner led the whole neighborhood in prayer for G.I. Joe and Lillie and their two children.

The block party raised over $900, and Lillie was so grateful to everybody. She needed the help. Her Blue Cross health insurance and what money she had left had run out at about the same time.

My Hero

In November, Lillie had a meeting with the doctors at the hospital.

"Joe is going to survive," they told Lillie, "but his right side will be paralyzed for life. And he will never be able to talk."

Lillie knew the days ahead would be difficult, although she was somewhat relieved.

They also felt that he needed to be hospitalized for a while so he could have access to physical and speech therapy. They all agreed that he would be transferred to the Veterans Hospital in Coatsville, Pennsylvania. He would be there for two years.

Joey got his license and drove Lillie to Coatsville on some Sundays. It took about an hour and a half each way. Sometimes, Lillie would take the bus alone.

Lillie only took Nancy one time. She went to pieces when she saw her father in that place, so Lillie never took her again.

"Over and over again, our family was severely tested," Lillie said later, "but together and with God's help, we made it work. I thanked God every night for my two wonderful kids, and I prayed for hours for my husband."

G.I. Joe was rehabilitated to the point where he could eventually know and recognize his family. He would cry and do his best to let them know that he was sorry.

Lillie would just hold him in her arms.

"I loved him; he was my husband," she said. "He was a hero."

Just as God has promised us, "I will never leave thee, nor forsake thee," Lillie stayed with G.I. Joe. For some people, the easy way out might be to walk out and start over again with someone else. But not for Lillie — she was standing on the promises of God.

Don't Take My Son!

By the summer of 1966, the Vietnam War was raging and Joey was drafted. He and his mother stood before the draft board in an upper floor office on Allegheny Avenue four blocks from home.

Lillie made the case that Joey was needed at home. "We just can't get along without him," she pleaded.

The board considered the case while Joey and Lillie sat outside on a bench. Lillie prayed to herself, "God, please don't let them take my son."

After the family was called back inside, they took a seat at the end of a long rectangular table. A man in the uniform of the U.S. Army stood up and began to speak.

"A Bronze, a Silver, and a Purple Heart with two oak leaf clusters. That means three Purple Hearts. A hero.

"And you," he pointed at Lillie, "a WAC who, among your many duties, found the time to escort the wounded home after the war."

He sat down. "Your family has done enough for this nation, ma'am. Your son is designated 3-A — hardship, sole support!

"Next case."

G.I. Joe kept his promise to his son. Because of his dad's stroke, Joey would never see "that hell!"

In January of 1967, G.I. Joe came home. For one weekend each month, he would undergo more rehabilitation as an outpatient at either the Veterans Hospital in Wilmington, Delaware, or up north at the Veterans Rehabilitation Center in East Orange, New Jersey. Joey always drove them to these sessions.

Joey wrecked the station wagon, so Lillie signed a note for him to help buy a 1959 "winged monster" Chevrolet Impala. G.I. Joe liked this car. It was certainly nicer than anything he had ever driven.

The winged monster knew the way to the veterans' facilities. After about 15 months of this, the VA doctors said that he would never get any better, so they released him for good into Lillie's care.

Lillie's Kids

Over the coming years, Lillie's kids grew up and moved away from Jasper Street. Although neither

G.I. Joe and Lillie in the late sixties.

of them went to college, both would become very successful.

Nancy went to flight attendant school and worked in public relations for WFIL-TV and radio. Years later she graduated from a cosmetology and barber school and went on to become one of the most popular hair designers in Philadelphia.

Joey struggled throughout his twenties but persevered and eventually made a good enough living that he was able to send money home to his parents every month. The extra money supplemented the Social Security benefits and the meager veterans checks.

☆
☆
☆

"Joey's money helped to pay for the little extras," Lillie said.

Lillie loved her children both the same and always encouraged them to work hard and to honor God in all they did.

Joey would come back home and visit whenever possible. Nancy lived only a few minutes away in Cherry Hill, New Jersey, and she remained close to her mother.

Joey eventually married and often brought his family home to visit his parents.

Nancy never married. She was always successful in whatever she did and was a constant friend and helper to her mother. Both kids seemed to have Lillie's incredible energy and personality. They also possessed their father's courage and pure grit.

Aging Together

Lillie worked for years at the Craftex Mill and took care of G.I. Joe. She would run home on lunch breaks to make sure that he was all right. G.I. Joe and Lillie proceeded to age together right there at 3517 Jasper Street.

For several years, G.I. Joe was able to walk with a cane, but eventually he was confined to a wheelchair. The condition of his leg became worse and worse, and his right arm was completely useless to him. He could only say about 15 words. How ironic it was that his good side was the side wounded in battle.

The Veterans' Administration never abandoned G.I.

Joe. They did, of course, have Lillie to contend with on a regular basis. They took care of most all of G.I. Joe's needs, including a new wheelchair, a lift for the front steps, checkups, evaluations, and other medical needs.

Once in a while, a team of army doctors would arrive at Jasper Street to remove more shrapnel from various parts of his body.

G.I. Joe's mother, Eleanor, only came to the house and visited him one time after his stroke. He cried and cried over seeing his mother. She fell asleep on the couch for an hour and then went home without ever saying much to him. When she passed away in 1969, Lillie did not tell G.I. Joe about it.

Their Own Little Universe

Eventually, Lillie was not able to continue working, and spent all of her time looking after Joe.

Joey would come home and take G.I. Joe to a Phillies game or to a movie. Sometimes he would take his parents out to eat or drive them down to "da shore" to look at the ocean. Joey and his father would often sit in the tiny kitchen at home and play seven-card stud with deuces wild until the sun came up. G.I. Joe usually won, too.

Nancy continued to make sure that her mother had everything she needed. She was always running back and forth from her home in Cherry Hill, New Jersey, over the Betsy Ross Bridge to Jasper Street to look in on her mother.

G.I. Joe loved TV dinners, wrestling on TV, and the Phillies baseball club. Lillie loved banana splits and the Philadelphia Eagles football team. The couple argued constantly over food and sports. They lived in their own little universe right there on 3517 Jasper Street until the fall of 1998.

Lillie's dedication to this man never wavered, and her love for her God and family ran deep and seemed to have no end. As much as she loved her husband, she also felt sorry for him. She felt that, for the most part, he had been dealt a hand that he didn't deserve, and she felt somewhat duty bound to look after him.

Some things never changed over the years. G.I. Joe slept in a hospital bed in the living room and still had nightmares about the war. Lillie, who usually slept nearby on the couch, would hold him in her arms and sing to him.

"You see, he is my husband, and he fought the war. He is my hero. I won't throw him away like an old shoe!"

And she never did.

CHAPTER ELEVEN

TAKING CARE OF G.I. JOE

T he decision to leave Jasper Street and enter the "soldiers' home," rested entirely with Lillie. It always did.

The results of two rough childbirths, a plethora of operations in her younger years, working hard at several jobs, taking care of her husband, raising two kids, and fighting a constant battle with diabetes were all slowly taking their toll on Lillie's overall health.

In 1996, G.I. Joe took a fall and broke his hip. It was a tough year. He spent over nine months in a lower body cast. Looking after him through all of this was extremely draining, and Lillie knew that she couldn't handle it all much longer. She needed help now, and perhaps someone to take care of her as well as her husband.

The old neighborhood had become the victim of urban decay. The streets had gone downhill for years and were getting worse with the passing of time.

Many houses and old stores were now boarded up, and most of the people who lived in the neighborhood were not the same as before. The old neighbors were either long gone or dead.

North Philly had always been tough, but the situation that existed now was much worse. Gangs ruled over many of the streets, and drug abuse and all sorts of crime ran rampant. It was becoming a much more dangerous place in which to live.

Joey had installed a very sophisticated home protection system in the house, and Nancy called almost every day. Still, they worried constantly about G.I. Joe and Lillie.

For well over a decade both kids had tried to convince Lillie to move to a small house in Jersey or out in the suburbs. She would not hear of it! "I worked hard to pay off this house, and I will not leave it until I say that it is time," she told them repeatedly.

G.I. Joe and Lillie were getting closer to that "time" with each passing day. Lillie had lost quite a bit of her eyesight and was giving herself insulin shots three times a day. Doctors and nurses were constantly coming in and out of the little row house in Kensington.

Leaving Home

Two scary diabetic comas tipped the scales in favor of the "soldiers' home." Lillie's inability to see, together with the wrong diet and not taking her shots when she should, all worked together to throw her body's chemistry into unpredictable stroke-like events.

God was looking after her because, on each of these occasions, someone else besides G.I. Joe was in the house. The first time, a nurse from the Veterans Administration was present. At another time the man who delivered oxygen recognized that Lillie needed help.

Had they been alone, Lillie would not have survived these attacks. She realized that if she had died, there would be no one to take care of her husband.

Lillie worked out all of the details for her and G.I. Joe to leave Jasper Street and enter the Southeastern Pennsylvania Veterans Center in Spring City, just outside of Royersford, Pennsylvania.

Overall, the move made sense. They were in their seventies and both needed constant care. Lillie did not want to go to another kind of retirement facility or nursing home. She didn't trust them to look after her and G.I. Joe, but she knew the Veterans Center would treat them both with the kind of respect that they deserved. To her, it was like being back in the army, and that made her feel safe and secure.

She was certainly right about that.

On a beautiful day in late September of 1998, Joey and Nancy came to escort their parents to their new home. They brought an ambulance with them to transport G.I. Joe. Lillie climbed in the back so she could ride with him on their last trip down Jasper Street.

Joey and Nancy road together in silence in Nancy's little gray Saturn as they followed the ambulance out of Philadelphia and toward upstate Pennsylvania.

They couldn't find one word to say to each other during this very strange and surreal journey, so they just held hands and wept all the way to the "soldiers' home," as Lillie called the Veteran's Center.

Ball Games and Bingo

G.I. Joe and Lillie's pictures were displayed on the door of room 411. Their matching beds faced one another. Their wedding picture as well as other family photos adorned the four walls.

G.I. Joe's medals were neatly and proudly displayed in a wooden case that now hung above his bed. This was Lillie's idea and, for once, her husband didn't seem to mind.

The *Philadelphia Inquirer* even sent a reporter out to do a story on them. It was a human-interest piece that ran in the Sunday supplement of the paper, complete with a wonderful picture of G.I. Joe kissing Lillie on the cheek.

They ate well and, more importantly, they were treated well. Their every need was administered to

24 hours a day, seven days a week, by a staff of doctors, nurses, orderlies, administrators, and volunteer workers who cared about the veterans.

For entertainment, they were taken on field trips to ball games and concerts as well as excursions to the Wal-Mart Supercenter. There were plenty of activities like bingo on Thursdays and church every Sunday morning. Lillie received her insulin shots on time, and banana splits were not allowed!

Room 411

The Last "Home"

Everyone seemed to love G.I. Joe and Lillie. The staff as well as the other vets at the center had a lot of respect for both of them. Lillie was appreciated for her years of dedication to her God, her country, and her husband. G.I. Joe, of course, was admired for the medals that hung above his bed.

There was just one small problem. For the most part, G.I. Joe hated the place. He could never figure out why he was there instead of home. On some level he realized that Lillie was not able to care for him like she used to, but he still believed that he should be in his own bed and not in a strange facility.

Old veterans

In the middle of the night he continued to be tormented by the nightmares that had haunted him for years. There in the darkness of room 411, he would wake up in the middle of the night and weep like a little baby. Lillie would go to him, hold him, kiss him, and tell him how much she loved him. Then she would rock him back to sleep.

When Joey came to visit one weekend, G.I. Joe made his case to his son by using only one word — "home." That was a word that his father could say, and Joey knew exactly what he meant.

Joey tried to explain to his father why he was at the soldiers' home and why Lillie needed the nurses' care because of her diabetes and overall poor health.

"Mom is very sick," Joey said. "This is really the place where you should be, Pop. It's best for you and for Mom."

Joey didn't tell him that Nancy had sold the house on Jasper Street and that this was the last "home" that he would ever know. It was downright heartbreaking.

The Great Escape

G.I. Joe was old and frail with few communication skills. He was paralyzed on one side and could not get in and out of bed without being hoisted like a sack of potatoes. He couldn't even go to the bathroom anymore without help.

In spite of his disabilities, the old Tough Ombre of the 90th Infantry Division still managed to escape from the Southeastern Pennsylvania Veterans Center.

G.I. Joe knew how to handle a wheelchair. By using his left arm on the left wheel and pushing off with his left foot (yes, the wounded one), he could make his way to the elevator every morning. He would go down to the first floor, wave at the guard, and go outside.

Many veterans did this. It was a way to get some fresh air. The men would sit in their wheel chairs or on the park benches and smoke and talk about the old days.

Beyond the sitting area was the Veterans Center parking lot. If you turned left out of the lot, you ended up at the U.S. Army National Guard base. If you turned right, the road climbed a very steep hill. At the top of the hill you made a right turn and then a left at the stop sign.

The two-lane blacktop then led away from the complex and into Spring City. In town, there was a bridge by a Wendy's restaurant that went into the nearby town of Royersford. This is where they found G.I. Joe, still wheeling, three miles from the "soldiers' home."

No one could figure out how he accomplished this incredible feat. What he did was physically impossible.

When the police car containing the commandant himself pulled up along side of Joe, he was laughing out loud!

"Where are you going, Joe?" he asked.

"I dunno," muttered G.I. Joe with a smile on his face. That day he had more fun than when he stole the army tank many years ago.

If he had been able to communicate properly, he probably would have said, "I thought I'd head into Philly and find my old house. Why do you ask?"

The situation could have been funnier except for the fact that G.I. Joe found himself in a whirlwind of trouble over this little escapade.

The psychologists thought that he was now a bit crazy and perhaps dangerous as well.

Their conclusion was, "The man escaped and might do it again, or he might bring harm to himself or others."

In order to determine G.I. Joe's mental state, the psychologists sent him to the Pottstown Hospital for evaluation.

Lillie was fit to be tied.

Going Home

"They think he is crazy, Joey," Lillie said when she phoned her son.

"They just don't understand him. You have to come here and do something!"

"I'll be there tomorrow, Mom," he replied.

Joey phoned the staff at the Veteran's Center and called for a meeting the next afternoon.

With Lillie and Nancy by his side, he pleaded the case on behalf of G.I. Joe. "The man is not crazy, he was just homesick. He must come back here. The tests must stop. He doesn't understand why this is happening."

"We agree with you, son," the supervising physician of the center replied. "We all love him very much. I'll admit that he is a handful, but if you can convince the psychiatric staff at Pottstown to allow him to come back, we'll try to keep a better eye on him."

Joey drove on to Pottstown to talk with the doctors there.

When a man with a clipboard walked in and started to question his father, Joey was in the room.

After a few minutes went by, Joey asked, "Are you aware, sir, that my father cannot talk?"

The doctor paid no attention to Joey and kept badgering the old man.

"Sir, my father cannot talk," Joey said again.

"Cannot or *will* not?" asked the doctor, who was obviously annoyed over this uncooperative mental case lying in the bed.

"Sir, have you even looked at his records?" asked Joey.

"I have not," the doctor replied. "I just need to get a few solid answers if I am to properly evaluate this man."

"Sir, what floor are we on?" inquired the son of G.I. Joe.

"The eighth floor, I believe," he replied. "Why is that relevant?"

"It is relevant because I am going to throw you right out that window in ten seconds. One . . . two . . . three. . . ."

The doctor was gone in a flash, and father and son laughed out loud.

Within one hour, Joey had G.I. Joe discharged from Pottstown. An ambulance picked him up and took him back to the Veterans Center.

Lillie was so happy to see him, and the nurses gave him a homecoming party.

They never really had to worry much about G.I. Joe escaping again. He didn't have the strength to do something like that anymore. For the most part, he was now confined to his bed. But he still would rather have been at "home."

On January 27, 2001, G.I. Joe left the Veterans Center for good. He finally went "home."

CHAPTER TWELVE

NOBODY WORRY ABOUT ME!

G. I. Joe's body rested in a coffin in Macungie, Pennsylvania, a town that G.I. Joe had never been to in his life. The Boyko Funeral Home was small and very efficient. On the evening of January 30, 2001, Joe's family and several old veterans from the center paid their last respects.

G.I. Joe had always loved little singing animals, and his kids had provided him with lots of laughs over the years. In his collection was a singing fish, a karaoke mouse, a dancing ape that sang Elvis songs, and many others. His favorite was a gopher from the movie *Caddyshack* that twisted in place while singing the Kenny Loggins song, "I'm All Right."

153

After many tears and some kind words by an army chaplain, Nancy said, "If I may speak for a moment on behalf of my father. I think he would have wanted you all to know this," and she pushed the start button on the little gopher, who sang, "I'm all right, nobody worry about me!"

Everyone applauded, and Nancy placed the little toy inside the coffin. It was a precious and wonderful moment.

Later on, Joey sat at a desk in the rear of the funeral home removing G.I. Joe's medals from the wooden case and was placing them in a small carry bag. An old, half-blind veteran by the name of Louie shuffled up behind him.

G.I. Joe's medals

"I loved him, you know. Called him the general. He was a real piece of work, that guy!" Louie said softly.

He leaned closer to Joey. "Are those his medals?"

"Yes, sir," Joey replied.

"That guy must have given up a huge part of himself to bring home that kind of metal," Louie said as he walked away with tears running down both cheeks.

Yeah, that's right, Louie, Joey said to himself. *He paid for it over his entire life.*

Joey wept as he finished packing up the medals.

Arlington

On January 31, 2001, a small funeral procession made its way from upstate Pennsylvania to Arlington, Virginia. The body that rested under the flag was that of G.I. Joe. His body would be interred in the hallowed ground of Arlington National Cemetery.

His Silver Star, Bronze Star, and Purple Heart with two oak leaf clusters earned him the right to be buried and honored in this sacred place.

The stunning military funeral was complete with honor guard and a 21-gun salute. Joe was buried as a true American hero.

When they handed Lillie the folded flag "on behalf of a grateful nation," she actually smiled. She felt blessed in knowing that only his body now slept in Arlington. His soul now lived with Jesus, and his pain had ended.

(Photo by Steven M. Robinson)

Lillie looked hard and long at her children and grandchildren. Then she bowed her head and prayed.

Later that day, she said these words to her son. "Your father can talk now, and he can walk again. I just hope he stays out of trouble. When I get there, I wonder if God will let us go dancing?"

"I think he will, Mom," Joey responded. "God has a soft spot in His heart for old soldiers."

They both laughed.

Memorial Day

Four months later, on Memorial Day in May 2001, Joey, his wife, and sister Nancy drove Lillie from the Veterans Center to Arlington, Virginia.

Lillie wanted to visit his grave now that the grass had turned green and the flowers were blooming. During this day of remembrance, each grave displayed a small American flag. It was a beautiful sight with row upon row of snowy white headstones adorned in red, white, and blue stars and stripes.

Lillie, Nancy, and Joey visit G.I. Joe's grave.

As a light rain fell, Lillie sat in her wheelchair and stared at the tiny white marker. It was a beautiful and peaceful spot, and her children wondered what she was thinking.

Her health was failing by the day, and they feared that it wouldn't be long until their precious mother would be resting right here with their father.

As usual, she was concerned about her husband. There had been a rash of graveyard desecrations in eastern Pennsylvania, and she wanted to make sure that he was protected.

"Mom," Joey assured her. "This is the most protected cemetery in the world. The Army Old Guard watches over it day and night. Absolutely nothing bad can happen here."

They took her to watch the changing of the guard at the Tomb of the Unknowns to prove the point. Lillie couldn't see them very well, but she was nevertheless comforted by the appearance of the young soldiers in uniform.

(On September 11, 2001, a hijacked airliner crashed into the side of the Pentagon. Had it come up short, it would have landed right in the middle of Arlington National Cemetery. By then, Lillie was too sick to comprehend the awful events that changed all Americans forever. That was a blessing.)

On the trip home from visiting G.I. Joe's grave, Nancy thought that the drive back up Interstate 95 on such a dreary day could be livened up a bit if they would all sing.

Her idea was to think of songs with a color in them. Joey, his wife, and Nancy took turns coming up with songs like "Red River Valley," "Blue Velvet," and "Yellow Submarine."

They laughed and sang color songs for over an hour, but Lillie said nothing. "Blue Suede Shoes," "Black Is the Color of My True Love's Hair," "White Christmas." On and on they sang traveling up Interstate 95. After a while, the group ran out of songs, so they drove in silence towards Spring City, Pennsylvania.

All of a sudden, from the back seat, with perfect timing, Lillie sang out at the top of her lungs, "Ohhhhhhhhh, the old gray mare she ain't what she used to be, she ain't what she used to be, she ain't what she used to be!"

What an incredible woman!

Give My Best to the General

In the fall, Lillie's kidneys started to fail her. Joey flew in to see her every week, and his sister Nancy never left her bedside at the Phoenixville Hospital just six miles down the road from the Veterans Center.

Lillie was dying.

She told Joey, "I want to go back to the soldiers home so I can die there among the other veterans."

Joey made the arrangements.

Before the ambulance came to get Lillie, Nancy asked her mother, "Are you hungry?"

Lillie replied, "I would love a big, fat banana split, Honey."

Joey and Nancy took turns feeding Lillie every last bit of the largest banana split ever prepared on the East Coast.

When she was finished, she smiled and said, "That was delicious!"

Back in room 411, Lillie was propped up in an oversized wheelchair. Throughout the day a steady procession of veterans and staff came and sat by her side for a bit.

From time to time, Lillie would drift away and then awaken to greet more visitors.

Chaplains of three faiths came to pray with her. The Protestant minister held her hands and prayed with her, the Catholic father gave her last rites, and the rabbi sang a song softly into her ear in Hebrew.

G.I. Joe's friend Louie sat with her and wept. "Give my best to the general when you see him," he requested.

When everyone had left, Lillie led Joey and Nancy in a word of prayer. As usual, she prayed for her two kids whom she loved so much.

A beautiful example of a mother's pure love came on a night when Nancy was keeping vigil at her bedside.

Lillie woke up and asked, "Joey, are you here?"

Nancy took her hand and said, "Mommy, Joey is not here right now, but I am here."

Lillie smiled and whispered, "Same thing, Honey, same thing."

On October 23, 2001, almost nine months to the day of the passing of G.I. Joe, his dear wife of 55 years lost her battle with diabetes.

Lillie also went home to be with our Lord.

When the Bugle Has Sounded

In Arlington National Cemetery, close to the corner of Eisenhower and York, a huge and weathered oak tree seems to stand guard over the gravesites at the end of the row. Beneath its protective boughs, snowy white stones now mark the resting place of G.I. Joe and Lillie.

Back in the army once again, the husband and wife veterans are surrounded by fallen heroes who, like them, sacrificed a huge part of their lives to pay for the freedoms we enjoy today in the USA.

Their two children, Joey and Nancy, will sail their little ship upon much grayer waters until that promised day when they will gather on the "heavenly shore" and rejoice in the light of the Lord.

As I wrote in the beginning of this story, one can only imagine the place that God has prepared for the likes of them.

The guns are now silent. The bugle has sounded. All of the nightmares are over.

Let me hold you in my arms, handsome soldier
Take my hand for we are going home today
Let me kiss away your tears
Let me pray away your fears
I'll stay here with you
Until they carry us away

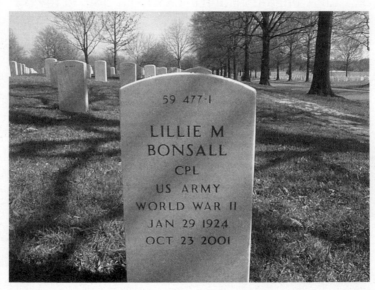

(Photo by Joseph S. Bonsall)

AN AMERICAN LOVE STORY

om would always say to me, "Son, are you ever going to write that book about me and your father?"

"Yes," I always promised.

I just wish that she had lived to see it.

If you have stuck with me to this point, then you may have already guessed that their son, Joey, is your author.

I want to thank you for reading this book. I am honored that you would take the time, and I pray that you have enjoyed the story of G.I. Joe and Lillie. I hope that it has been a blessing to your life. That, as well as honoring my parents, has been my constant goal in writing their story.

I am proud to say that my parents were Private First Class Joseph Sloan Bonsall Sr. of the United States Army and Corporal Lillie Maude Collins Bonsall, Women's Army Corps.

I believe that every life has a story and every story is important. I have found that people enjoy a true-life family story for many reasons.

On many levels, we are all a bit voyeuristic. Hanging out in someone else's house and watching them live their lives is always a bit exhilarating.

Whatever the reason, we all like to compare other folks' lives with our own. That is probably why reality TV shows and behind-the-scene magazines are so popular. I know that I have been hooked on the Biography Channel since its inception for many of these same reasons.

We also live in a new day and age in which many of America's past principles and treasured ideals have been sadly diminished. It is my prayer that the story of G.I. Joe and Lillie will be more of an inspiration than just a peek into someone else's life.

The good soldier who fought the war and the woman who loved him is a story as old as time itself. As we approach the uncertainties of the future, it is good to know that this kind of love, faith, and dedication does exist. Yes, I believe it does and, yes, I believe it always will.

The key word here is "faith" — faith in God, faith in country, faith in each other.

My mom always believed that God and her family came first. She was a woman of prayer — the "down on your knees for a long time" kind of prayer.

From the time Nancy and I were little, we would hear her praying. She would bow her head at any time of the day and thank God for His blessings.

When situations were as bad as they could possibly be, it was my mother's strength, character, and faith on a daily basis that let us know we were safe and that things would work out just fine.

It is hard to be afraid when you can hear your mother praying for you, even when your father has suffered a debilitating stroke.

Every single day, my mother told us, "I love you with all my heart." Nancy and I know that to be true.

I would not be singing on any stage today if not for my mother. She always taught me that if you treat people right, always tell the truth, be willing to sacrifice, and work hard, you *will* succeed.

My mother always reminded us: "Men like your father fought and died so that you could pursue your dreams. That is what living in America is all about."

Still Singing

I must tell you that Mommy and Daddy dearly loved the Oak Ridge Boys. They came to hear us sing over and over throughout the years.

Daddy's body rests in Arlington all dressed out in an Oak Ridge Boys t-shirt. An Oaks picture blanket with my face on top was buried with my mother.

Not long ago, I asked my sister Nancy, "Who do I sing for now? I always sang for her."

Nancy replied so sweetly, "You *still* sing for her, Joey."

Yes, I do, indeed.

In his later years, G.I. Joe became very close to God. He always let his kids know that he was sorry for the bad times and that he loved us.

Anyone who has lived with a handicapped person knows that, with real love and a bit of patience, you can understand his heart and get a handle on every word he tries to say.

Daddy had two phrases that were unmistakable: "Jeeeesus" and "I uv ooo, Honey." No need for a degree from Harvard to figure out those words.

I know that my parents are both dancing in heaven, holding on tightly to one another. What I don't know is how he ever made it through those nine months without her.

Before I start to say thank you to all of the good folks who made this project possible, I want to end this little epilogue by saying a special thank you to G.I. Joe and Lillie:

My precious Mother and Father, I miss you both so very much, and I love you with all of my heart. Here is your book. I will place a copy on your grave at Arlington. Please share it with the Gruenbaums, Nana Gertrude Clark, and all the other angels!

THANK YOU'S

I first wrote *G.I. Joe & Lillie* as a short story. I thought that it might make a good addition to a bowl of *Chicken Soup for the Veteran's Soul* or, at best, a similar book.

I owe much to Jim Fletcher and Roger Howerton and many others at New Leaf Press for taking a chance on this project.

My biggest "thank you" goes to the big guy, Tim Dudley, for his early vision and ideas. He was the one who saw *G.I. Joe & Lillie* as a much bigger story. "This needs to be a book," he said. "The story is wonderful, and the characters are real. People can be blessed by reading about this kind of love and dedication. Our country needs a story like this. I need a *big* book here. Can you do it?"

I will always be more than grateful to Tim for putting forth the challenge. God bless you, my friend.

I also want to thank a few other people who have made this book a reality. Things do not just happen. It always takes a team.

Thank you, Kathy Harris, my long-time friend and associate. She talked with Lillie for years about her story. "Some day I'm going to write a book," Lillie would say.

Kathy acted as my agent on this project. She persevered, in part, because she thought the book idea was good and the writing was worthy. She also had a heartfelt desire to see Lillie's dream come true as well. It was Kathy Harris who found a home for *G.I. Joe and Lillie* at New Leaf Press.

I thank my family for their constant love and support. My incredible and beautiful wife, Mary, my wonderful daughters, Jennifer and Sabrina, my hard-working sons-in-law, Dan and Mark, and my two lovely grandchildren, Breanne and Luke. I cannot exist without them.

Thanks and love to Ruthie, Mary's Mom, another woman who has been there! God bless you!

I thank my long-time singing partners in the Oak Ridge Boys, Duane Allen, William Lee Golden, and Richard Sterban.

Thank you for recording the song and thank you for all the joy that you brought my parents all of these years. God bless you, my dearest friends.

Thanks to my long-time friend and counselor, S. Gary Spicer, for encouraging my writing and enriching my life.

Thanks to my godfather, Jim Halsey, for believing in me and for always inspiring me on to greater achievements.

Thank you, Timmer Ground, for miles of support and friendship!

Thanks to all of my friends on the board at http://www.oakridgeboys.com. I know that you were all praying for me.

I want to honor my dear friend Holly Richardson, from Scottsdale, Arizona, for inspiration and help beyond measure. She is a fine writer in her own right and was a constant and consistent help to me from the very beginning of this project. So, Holly, for heart, help, and better grammar, I thank you! Go D'Backs!

Thanks to Nancy Casteel, my good friend at America Online for some Bonsall family research as well as some terrific World War II history websites. Nancy, you *are* the Internet.

Thank you to my good friend Steve Robinson. Steve understands all of this.

Words cannot express my heartfelt thank you to Jean Becker for your involvement in this project. You are a dear friend and a patriot, and I will love you forever!

A special thank you to my cousin Jo Ann, who told me early on, "You still have some good family left, right here!"

I know that, Jo Ann. We have *all* come a long way from the train house.

And last of all, I thank my precious sister, Nancy Marie Bonsall. No one has sacrificed more on behalf of our little family ship than she has. This book could not, and would not, have happened if not for you! Thanks for always being there when I could not be. Thank you for your input, my sweet little Bug, and thank you for saving all that stuff! I pray for you every day. I love you dearly, my sweet sister, with all of my heart!

A Special Thank You to Barbara Bush

Several years ago on a visit to the Bush compound on Walkers Point in Kennebunkport, Maine, the Oak Ridge Boys and our lovely wives found ourselves sitting around a dinner table with President George Herbert Walker Bush, #41, and our wonderful former first lady, Barbara.

The dishes had been cleared and dessert had been eaten. Mrs. Bush then asked each of us to take a moment and talk about our parents, which we did.

After telling a little bit of the story that you have just read, Mrs. Bush said, "Your mother is one remarkable woman."

I have never forgotten that moment. It was a precious time for each of us.

Lillie loved the Bushes and was so proud that her son and daughter-in-law Mary, as well as my singing partners, were friends of this prominent family. In fact, my mother told everyone. If someone would ask, "Hey, Lillie, how's Joey and the Boys?" the answer would more than likely be, "Oh, they are with the Bushes in Maine right now." (Even if it had been six months ago.)

When Daddy died, George and Barbara sent a wonderful floral arrangement. It was so moving to see old veterans pay respects to the flowers they sent. They saluted them, and some wept.

Not long before Mommy died, she asked me, "Do the Bushes know that I am dying?"

I was able to tell her, "Yes, indeed. They said, 'Tell your mother we send our love and will be praying for her.' " It made her smile.

Another beautiful floral arrangement from George and Barbara Bush stood tall over her grave in Arlington on the day we buried her. Lillie would have loved that.

I thank President Bush and Barbara for their positive influence on my entire family. I also thank them for their life of service to our country.

From my heart, I thank you, Mrs. Bush, for taking the time to write the foreword to this book. The memory of G.I. Joe and Lillie is honored beyond words by your contribution.

May God continue to bless you and your family, including your son, President George W. Bush, as he leads our great nation.

You are a remarkable woman.

An Addendum . . . January 26, 2003

Mommy's Voice

It is Super Bowl Sunday. The day the Plundering Herd defense of Tampa Bay dismantled the Oakland Raiders. I can't help thinking of Mom. Lillie loved NFL football and if she had known just how close her beloved Philadelphia Eagles had come to being in the big game, she would not have been able to contain herself, yet, alas, the Buccaneers of Tampa Bay put an end to that dream as well. The Eagles are ice fishing with the Tennessee Titans on this day.

It is a busy time for me. The Oak Ridge Boys have begun to hit the road hard. Our Red White and Blu-Blocker Tour will play over 160 dates in 2003 and we are also putting the finishing touches on our new COLORS album that will release in May of 2003. My song, "G.I. Joe and Lillie," will be a part of that project and for this, I feel honored.

I am also in the process of going over each final detail of this book with the fine folks at New Leaf Press. I have been in constant touch with editors and publicity departments as well as graphic artists as we examine each and every word and picture in the finalization process of the book. It is all very exciting and exhilarating for me because I know that very, very soon, I will actually hold this story in my hand as a real published book.

The game is over and I find myself once again reading through the final galley of *G.I. Joe & Lillie* and thinking of my mother. She had told me that she would always watch over my sister Nancy and I, and I have never had a reason to doubt her. I so wished that I could call her and run some of this stuff by her for her input and direction, but all I have left are memories, memoirs, and pictures.

I put the book aside and rummage through my desk drawer for one of those special marking pens when my fingers happen to brush across a small, square object. It is in the very back corner of the middle drawer. I wrap my hand around it and bring it into view and I almost lose my breath. I know what this is. It is a small Radio Shack talking picture frame that Mom gave me several years ago as a Christmas present.

I am gasping for air as I open it.

There she is . . . on the left side of the opening smiling at me. I stare at the little round button that says PLAY and I am afraid to push it. The battery inside is surely dead by now. Suppose I push it and nothing happens. Oh, I would love to hear her voice. She has been gone for a year and a half now. . . . I press PLAY!

"Hello Son. I just want you to know, um [a slight laugh here, so sweet] that I love you and I thank you for everything."

Her voice. My mother's voice. Thank You, sweet

Jesus, for this blessing. I will never forget this moment. I sat the little picture frame on the final galley of *G.I. Joe & Lillie* and went to bed. By now, you have read this book and I am sure that you love her, too.

God bless all of you . . . Joey.

A Special Tribute to Arlington National Cemetery

There is no greater honor than to be buried in the hallowed grounds of Arlington, and I am thankful to God on each and every day that my dear parents, G.I. Joe and Lillie, are at rest there in that sacred place.

My long-time friend and associate Steve Robinson accompanied my family to both funeral services, and we were all very moved by the experience. Steve, who owns an events management company called LogiCom, is also an accomplished writer.

After Daddy and Mommy were buried, Steve wrote the following piece about Arlington in their honor:

Friend, Good Night
By Steven M. Robinson

The streets around it do not betray what you are about to experience. The people who direct traffic are just that: men and women who tell people where they should go and not go.

Upon entering the gates, parking the car, and walking into the administration building, nothing indicates the true nature of this place. It is only when the visitor, trailing slowly behind the funeral coach, makes his way down the park's tree-lined streets that the sanctity of this place becomes clear. You notice the names that grace the street signs — names like Eisenhower and Halsey.

It is the sight of the simple white grave markers that file far into the distance, however, that the stunned visitor cannot escape. The gardens of stone make their own stark statement, showcasing the enormity of the price paid for our freedom.

The falling leaves of gold and red ride the wind across the fields of green and past the smaller signs, which read simply: "Silence and respect."

Soldiers in dress uniforms march along the streets. As the visitor wonders who they are or why they are there, you notice that their marching abruptly ceases.

As the hearse that you follow slowly passes the group of anonymous soldiers, they stop, turn to face it, and snap a salute, which they hold until the fallen one passes. Then they turn and resume their marching.

This happens again and again. No living soldier on this hallowed ground, bursting with so many fallen soldiers, allows a newly fallen comrade to pass without the show of proper respect.

One wonders, is this merely a diversion from their other duties, or is their duty and their marching simply a diversion?

As the procession slows, your attention is drawn to a group of eight soldiers standing some 30 yards away. Seven of these bear arms. One holds a sword. Another 20 yards from this group is a solitary soldier, right arm fixed in salute, a bugle in his left hand.

The cortege reaches its destination. It is met by another group of soldiers, standing silently beneath a large oak tree with golden leaves bursting forth in a canopy of protection. Seven soldiers stand at attention in dress black pants and brilliant blue jackets with polished brass buttons and medals adorning each chest. Another soldier accompanies them. This one, older and more distinguished, wears the same uniform but with more medals and two shiny silver crosses on his lapels.

The rear door of the funeral coach is opened to reveal a flag-draped coffin. Silently, except for the tap of their polished shoes on the pavement, the group of seven makes its way to their fallen comrade.

Mechanically, yet reverently, six of them retrieve the coffin from its temporary home in three precise movements. You sense that they see the process as a rescue of sorts. They recognize this as a fallen comrade who is not yet at rest and will not be until they make it so.

With the fallen soldier safely in hand, the six escorts slowly march toward the hallowed ground that has been prepared to receive this honored one.

☆
☆
☆

When the flag-draped carrier is placed above its final resting-place, the six remove the flag, tightly holding it above in their white-gloved hands. The seventh, too, stands near. They all stand guard, at alert attention, over this grave as if it holds their own fallen commander.

Who are these men-boys? They are so young, so unfamiliar, and yet they seem so affected by their task, as if they are fortunate to have the duty of this honor.

History tells us they are members of the Third United States Infantry Regiment, the famed "Old Guard," one of the oldest and most respected infantry regiments in the United States Army. Perhaps they are chosen for their ability to respect or, more likely, their solemnity is earned through their duty.

The older soldier, the chaplain with crosses on his lapel, steps forward and says words chosen to comfort. He speaks from the heart, not from notes. He sees it as his duty and responsibility to speak of the fallen one as someone he knew. He does not pretend that he did. The chaplain simply knows the soldier's character because of those who sit before him and because of the right they have earned to be in this sacred place.

After a few words, the soldier in the distance who holds the silver sword directs his charges to honor the fallen one with the ultimate military salute. On his command, the remaining seven present their arms and each fires simultaneously. This action is repeated twice, comprising a salute of 21 guns, though not considered an official 21-gun salute. Such an honor is reserved for fallen Commanders-in-Chief.

This practice of firing volleys over the grave originated on the battlefields of yesterday. Fighting would cease while each army cleared away its fallen. After the dead had been removed and cared for, each army would fire three volleys to signal that the fighting could resume — an odd sort of respect on a field of conflict.

On this hallowed ground, it strikes you that these volleys symbolize the opposite. This gunfire signals that the dead is again cared for but, for the fallen soldier, all fighting has come to an honorable end.

As quickly as the sound of gunfire came, it retreats — now replaced with the mournful strains of that most familiar of military melodies.

Day is done, gone the sun,
From the lake, from the hills, from the sky.
All is well, safely rest, God is nigh.

As silence again fills the chilly air, the six, who watch over the grave solemnly, without even blinking and barely breathing, snap the flag taut while reverently folding it into the triangle of blue and white stars. This procedure takes a few minutes, not because they are unfamiliar with the process but because they intimately know, not only the *how* of what they are doing but also the *why*.

This flag represents the nation, as does any other American flag. This one, however, has graced the coffin of a fallen hero. As significant as that is to the defense of the country, it is even more important for the family member to whom it will be presented. To him or her, the flag not only graced the coffin of a fallen hero, it graced the coffin of a fallen loved one.

The flag is presented by one of the six soldiers to the seventh, who has stood watch on their service. He then presents it to the chaplain, who has the honor and the duty to present the flag to the fallen one's next-of-kin: "This flag is presented on behalf of the President of the United States, and a grateful nation, as a token of appreciation for the honorable and faithful service rendered by your loved one."

He then presents the Lady of Arlington, one of about 60 volunteers who attend every funeral that occurs in this sacred place. "No one worthy of this place should be buried alone." That was the genesis of Arlington's Ladies.

This lady, escorted by yet another member of the Old Guard, represents the leadership of the branch of service in which the fallen one served. She speaks a few words of comfort to the family and then presents a letter of appreciation and condolence acknowledging that the fallen one has found his final resting-place.

As the service ends, the family returns to their cars. As they depart, they are honored with one more long, slow salute from each of the soldiers, all of whom now line the street.

The family will attempt to return to life while these fine members of the Old Guard will return to their duty of honoring America's fallen. Their paths will likely never cross again, but that's all right. We are better for having known they were there for us and that they will be there for others.

The history of the cemetery tells us that "since 1864, when the first coffin was interred, more than 200,000 burials have taken place in the more than 600 acres of land devoted to America's honored dead. Privates and generals, astronauts and presidents, civilians with military service or relationships are all ranked in row upon row in the manicured lawns. By the year 2021 the cemetery will be full, and the burial ground will be designated a national shrine."

☆
☆
☆

This fine line of legalese will change nothing for the families of those whose loved ones rest here. What began as hallowed ground is now made even more so by the presence of their mothers, their fathers, their sons, and their daughters.

> Then good night, peaceful night,
> Till the light of the dawn shineth bright,
> God is near, do not fear —
> Friend, good night.

S.M.R.

The written memoirs of Lillie M. Bonsall.

A History of the 90th Division in World War Two (Nashville, TN: Battery Press).

Jonathan Gawne, *Spearheading D-Day: American Special Units of the Normandy Invasion* (Paris: Histoire & Collections, 1998).

Stephen E. Ambrose, *Eisenhower: Soldier and President* (New York, NY: Simon and Schuster, 1990).

Stephen E. Ambrose, *Band of Brothers* (New York, NY: Simon and Schuster, 1992).

Normandy 6 June to 24 July, 1944, U.S. Army Military Archives.

Judith A. Bellafaire, *The Women's Army Corps: A Commemoration of World War II Service* (online at http://www.army.mil/cmh-pg/brochures/wac/wac.htm)

Ninetieth Division, © Copyright 1999, 2000
http://www.grunts.net

OTHER ONLINE RESEARCH

Arlington National Cemetery
http://www.arlingtoncemetery.com

Steven M. Robinson:
http://www.logicomonline.com

NARA/US National Archives & Records Administration
http://www.archives.gov/

The United States Army Homepage
http://www.army.mil

The Woman's Army Corp
http://www.army.mil/cmh-pg/brochures/wac/wac.htm

The 90th Infantry Division
http://www.army.mil/cmh-pg/brochures/wac/wac.htm

Association Normandy 44 - 90th US Division
http://assoc.wanadoo.fr/normandy44-90div.us/usa/

Military.com remembers D-Day
http://216.239.35.100/search?q=cache:h0GMXsKiu
WIC:www.military.com/Content/MoreContent1/
%3Ffile%3Ddday_0021p1+90th++infantry+division&hl=
en&ie=UTF-8

Mitchel Field
http://www.hempsteadplains.com/

Fort Dix
http://www.dix.army.mil/

Fort Hood
http://www.hood.army.mil/

Rosie the Riveter
http://womenshistory.about.com/gi/dynamic/offsite.
htm?site=http%3A%2F%2Fwww.goordnance.apg.army.mil
%2Frosie.htm

http://www.armywomen.org/

Master Index of Army Records
http://www.army.mil/cmh-pg/reference/records.htm

D-day Museum Online.
http://www.ddaymuseum.org

Welcome to Fort Meade, Maryland
http://www.ftmeade.army.mil/

Shaw Air Force Base Public Web Site
http://www.shaw.af.mil/default.htm

Utah Beach to Cherbourg 6 June–24 July 1944
Department of the Army Historical Division
http://www.army.mil/cmh-pg/books/wwii/utah/
utah.htm

The 90th "Battle Babies"
http://users.pandora.be/dave.depickere/Text/90th.html

The Internet Movie Database
http://www.imdb.com/

Military World: Veterans Information
http://www.militaryworld.com

Arlington National Cemetery
http://www.arlingtoncemetery.com

COMING SUMMER 2003!

The music of COLORS epitomizes everything

the Oak Ridge Boys have been about

in their 30 years of making music together . . .

faith, family, friends

& freedom

Join the Oaks as they celebrate

the ideals on which this great

country was founded,

with their new recording,

COLORS!